Advanced React

deep dives, investigations, performance patterns and techniques

by Nadia Makarevich

Illustrations and book cover design: Nadia Makarevich
Technical review: Andrew Grischenko

Table Of Contents

Chapter 14. Data fetching on the client and performance

Chapter 15. Data fetching and race conditions

Chapter 16. Universal error handling in React

Introduction: how to read this book

React is one of the most popular front-end frameworks out there. There is no arguing about that. As a result, the internet is filled with courses, books, and blogs about React. Also, the newly released documentation is very good. So, what is the point of this book? Is there even a gap it can fill?

I believe there is. I have been writing a blog dedicated to advanced patterns for React developers (https://www.developerway.com) for a while now. One of the most consistent pieces of feedback I receive is that there is not enough advanced-level content.

The docs are very good to start with React. Millions of books, courses, and blogs are out there aimed at beginners. But what to do after you've started successfully? Where to go if you want to understand how things work on a deeper level? What to read if you've been writing React for a while and beginner or even intermediate-level courses are not enough? There are not many resources available for this. This is the gap this book aims to fill.

The book assumes a certain basic knowledge of React. It expects you to understand what the state is and how to use it. What hooks are and how to write them. What a component is and how to render components inside other components. In other words, it assumes that you can successfully write a basic "todo" app.

What it aims to provide is the knowledge that allows you to progress from the "basic app" to "React guru in my team". It begins right away with investigating and fixing a performance bug. It digs deep into what re-renders are and how they affect performance. Walks you through how the reconciliation algorithm works, how to deal with closures in React, various composition patterns that can replace memoization, how memoization works, how to implement debouncing correctly, and much more.

The book is structured into chapters. Each chapter is an independent story, investigation, or deep dive focusing on a single topic. However, they are not completely isolated: each chapter builds on the knowledge introduced in the previous chapters. Also, each chapter tries to introduce only the knowledge required to understand the discussed concept, no more. To make the reading easier and more focused. It's no use, for example, to start with introducing the reconciliation algorithm in order to understand what a re-render is and how it affects performance.

So, I recommend reading the book in the order of the chapters. If your knowledge already extends beyond the simple "todo" app, it's very likely that you'll know a lot of the concepts already. For this case, every chapter has a bullet-point list of things you can expect to learn from it at the beginning, and a "Key takeaways" section, with a very short bullet-point summary of the things introduced. Just skimming through these first will give you a good idea of what's inside.

Lastly, I don't differentiate between `react`, `react-dom` and the JSX transpiler in the book. Technically, it's the `react-dom` library that is responsible for things like Portals, and transpilers such as Babel convert JSX syntax into functions. However, for understanding the content of the book, this distinction doesn't really matter. We use all three without even noticing when writing interfaces for the web. Therefore, for simplicity, everything is referred to as "React".

Hope you're ready to start now! We'll investigate a performance problem right away, learn the big re-renders myth, and look into the simplest but very powerful performance optimization pattern with composition. Ready? Let's get started!

Chapter 1. Intro to re-renders

Let's dive right in, shall we? And let's talk about performance right away: it's one of the most important topics these days when it comes to building applications, and as a result, it's an overarching theme of this book.

And when it comes to React and performance in React, it's crucial to understand re-renders and their influence. How they are triggered, how they propagate through the app, what happens when a component re-renders and why, and why we need them in the first place.

This chapter introduces these concepts, which will be explored in more detail in the next few chapters. And to make it more fun, let's make it in the form of an investigation. Let's introduce a very common performance problem in an app, look at what's happening because of it, and how to fix it with a very simple composition technique. While doing so, you will learn:

- What a re-render is, and why we need it.
- What the initial source of all re-renders is.
- How React propagates re-renders through the app.
- The big re-renders myth and why props changing by themselves doesn't matter.
- The "moving state down" technique to improve performance.
- Why hooks can be dangerous when it comes to re-renders.

The problem

Imagine yourself as a developer who inherited a large, complicated, and very performance-sensitive app. Lots of things are happening there, many people have worked on it over the years, millions of customers are using it now. As your first task on the job, you are asked to add a simple button that opens a modal dialog right at the top of this app.

You look at the code and find the place where the dialog should be triggered:

```
const App = () => {
  // lots of code here
  return (
    <div className="layout">
      {/* button should go somewhere here */}
      <VerySlowComponent />
      <BunchOfStuff />
      <OtherStuffAlsoComplicated />
    </div>
  );
};
```

Then you implement it. The task seems trivial. We've all done it hundreds of times:

```
const App = () => {
  // add some state
  const [isOpen, setIsOpen] = useState(false);

  return (
    <div className="layout">
      {/* add the button */}
      <Button onClick={() => setIsOpen(true)}>
        Open dialog
      </Button>
      {/* add the dialog itself */}
      {isOpen ? (
        <ModalDialog onClose={() => setIsOpen(false)} />
      ) : null}
      <VerySlowComponent />
      <BunchOfStuff />
      <OtherStuffAlsoComplicated />
    </div>
  );
};
```

Just add some state that holds whether the dialog is open or closed. Add the button that triggers the state update on click. And the dialog itself that is rendered if the state variable is `true`.

You start the app, try it out - and oops. It takes almost a second to open that simple dialog!

Interactive example and full code
https://advanced-react.com/examples/01/01

People experienced with dealing with React performance might be tempted to say something like: "Ah, of course! You're re-rendering the whole app there, you just need to wrap everything in `React.memo` and use `useCallback` hooks to prevent it." And technically this is true. But don't rush. Memoization is completely unnecessary here and will do more harm than good. There is a more efficient way.

But first, let's review what exactly is happening here and why.

State update, nested components, and re-renders

Let's start from the beginning: the life of our component and the most important stages of it that we need to care about when we talk about performance. Those are: mounting, unmounting, and re-rendering.

When a component first appears on the screen, we call it **mounting**. This is when React creates this component's instance for the first time, initializes its state, runs its hooks, and appends elements to the DOM. The end result - we see whatever we render in this component on the screen.

Then, there is **unmounting**: this is when React detects that a component is not needed anymore. So it does the final clean-up, destroys this component's instance and everything associated with it, like the component's state, and finally removes the DOM element associated with it.

And, finally, **re-rendering**. This is when React updates an already existing component with some new information. Compared to mounting, re-rendering is lightweight: React just re-uses the already existing instance, runs the hooks, does all the necessary calculations, and updates the existing DOM element with the new attributes.

Every re-render starts with the **state**. In React, every time we use a hook like `useState`, `useReducer`, or any of the external state management libraries like Redux, we add interactivity to a component. From now on, a component will have a piece of data that is preserved throughout its lifecycle. If something happens that needs an interactive response, like a user clicking a button or some external data coming through, we update the state with the new data.

Re-rendering is one of the most important things to understand in React. This is when React updates the component with the new data and triggers all the hooks that depend on that data. Without these, there will be no data updates in React and, as a result, no interactivity. The app will be completely static. And state update is the initial source of all re-renders in React apps. If we take our initial app as an example:

```
const App = () => {
  const [isOpen, setIsOpen] = useState(false);

  return (
    <Button onClick={() => setIsOpen(true)}>
      Open dialog
    </Button>
  );
};
```

When we click on the `Button`, we trigger the `setIsOpen` setter function: we update the `isOpen` state with the new value from `false` to `true`. As a result, the `App` component that holds that state re-renders itself.

After the state is updated and the `App` component re-renders, the new data needs to be delivered to other components that depend on it. React does this automatically for us: it grabs all the components that the initial component renders inside, re-renders those, then re-renders components nested inside of them, and so on until it reaches the end of the chain of components.

If you imagine a typical React app as a tree, everything down from where the state update was initiated will be re-rendered.

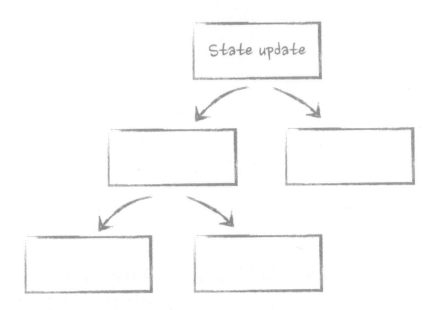

In the case of our app, everything that it renders, all those very slow components, will be re-rendered when the state changes:

```
const App = () => {
  const [isOpen, setIsOpen] = useState(false);

  // everything that is returned here will be re-rendered when the
state is updated
  return (
    <div className="layout">
      <Button onClick={() => setIsOpen(true)}>
        Open dialog
      </Button>
      {isOpen ? (
```

```
      <ModalDialog onClose={() => setIsOpen(false)} />
      ) : null}
      <VerySlowComponent />
      <BunchOfStuff />
      <OtherStuffAlsoComplicated />
    </div>
  );
};
```

As a result, it takes almost a second to open the dialog - React needs to re-render everything before the dialog can appear on the screen.

The important thing to remember here is that React never goes "up" the render tree when it re-renders components. If a state update originated somewhere in the middle of the components tree, only components "down" the tree will re-render.

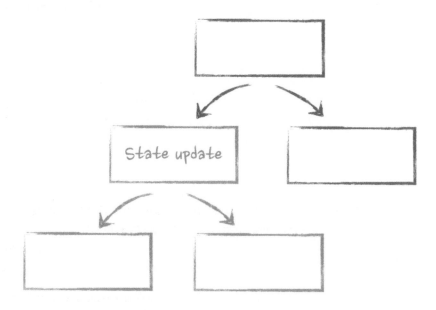

The only way for components at the "bottom" to affect components at the "top" of the hierarchy is for them either to explicitly call state update in the "top" components or to pass components as functions.

The big re-renders myth

Have you noticed that I haven't mentioned anything about props here? You might have heard this statement: **"Component re-renders when its props change."** It's one of the most common misconceptions in React: everyone believes it, no one doubts it, and it's just not true.

Normal React behavior is that if a state update is triggered, React will re-render all the nested components regardless of their props. And if a state update is not triggered, then changing props will be just "swallowed": React doesn't monitor them.

If I have a component with props, and I try to change those props without triggering a state update, something like this:

```
const App = () => {
  // local variable won't work
  let isOpen = false;

  return (
    <div className="layout">
      {/* nothing will happen */}
      <Button onClick={() => (isOpen = true)}>
        Open dialog
      </Button>
      {/* will never show up */}
      {isOpen ? (
        <ModalDialog onClose={() => (isOpen = false)} />
      ) : null}
    </div>
  );
};
```

It just won't work. When the `Button` is clicked, the local `isOpen` variable will change. But the React lifecycle is not triggered, so the render output is never updated, and the `ModalDialog` will never show up.

Interactive example and full code

In the context of re-renders, whether props have changed or not on a component matters only in one case: if the said component is wrapped in the `React.memo` higher-order component. Then, and only then, will React stop its natural chain of re-renders and first check the props. If none of the props change, then re-renders will stop there. If even one single prop changes, they will continue as usual.

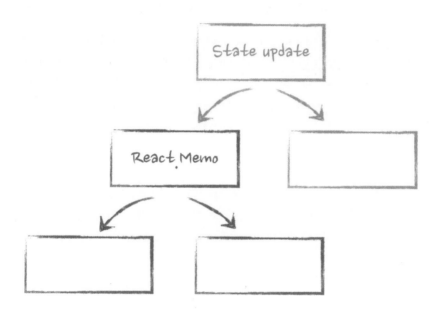

Preventing re-renders with memoization properly is a complicated topic with several caveats. Read about it in more detail in *Chapter 5. Memoization with useMemo, useCallback and React.memo.*

Moving state down

Now that it's clear how React re-renders components, it's time to apply this knowledge to the original problem and fix it. Let's take a closer look at the code, in particular where we use the modal dialog state:

```
const App = () => {
  // our state is declared here
  const [isOpen, setIsOpen] = useState(false);

  return (
    <div className="layout">
      {/* state is used here */}
      <Button onClick={() => setIsOpen(true)}>
        Open dialog
      </Button>
      {/* state is used here */}
      {isOpen ? (
        <ModalDialog onClose={() => setIsOpen(false)} />
      ) : null}
      <VerySlowComponent />
      <BunchOfStuff />
      <OtherStuffAlsoComplicated />
    </div>
  );
};
```

As you can see, it's relatively isolated: we use it only on the `Button` component and in `ModalDialog` itself. The rest of the code, all those very slow components, doesn't depend on it and therefore doesn't actually *need* to re-render when this state changes. It's a classic example of what is called an *unnecessary re-render*.

Wrapping them in `React.memo` will prevent them from re-rendering in this case, this is true. But `React.memo` has many caveats and complexities around it (see more in *Chapter 5. Memoization with useMemo, useCallback and React.memo*). There is a better way. All that we need to do is to extract components that depend on that state and the state itself into a smaller component:

```
const ButtonWithModalDialog = () => {
  const [isOpen, setIsOpen] = useState(false);

  // render only Button and ModalDialog here
  return (
    <>
```

```
    <Button onClick={() => setIsOpen(true)}>
      Open dialog
    </Button>
    {isOpen ? (
      <ModalDialog onClose={() => setIsOpen(false)} />
    ) : null}
  </>
  );
};
```

And then just render this new component in the original big `App`:

```
const App = () => {
  return (
    <div className="layout">
      {/* here it goes, component with the state inside */}
      <ButtonWithModalDialog />
      <VerySlowComponent />
      <BunchOfStuff />
      <OtherStuffAlsoComplicated />
    </div>
  );
};
```

> **Interactive example and full code**
> https://advanced-react.com/examples/01/03

Now, the state update when the `Button` is clicked is still triggered, and some components re-render because of it. But! It only happens with components inside the `ButtonWithModalDialog` component. And it's just a tiny button and the dialog that should be rendered anyway. The rest of the app is safe.

Essentially, we just created a new sub-branch inside our render tree and moved our state down to it.

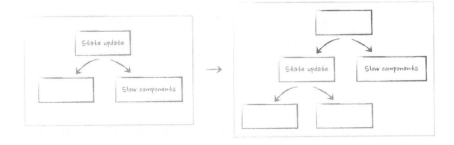

As a result, the modal dialog appears instantly. We just fixed a big performance problem with a simple composition technique!

The danger of custom hooks

Another very important concept that we should not forget when dealing with state, re-renders, and performance is custom hooks. After all, they were introduced exactly so that we could abstract away stateful logic. It's very common to see logic like the one we had above extracted into something like the `useModalDialog` hook. A simplified version could look like this:

```
const useModalDialog = () => {
  const [isOpen, setIsOpen] = useState(false);

  return {
    isOpen,
    open: () => setIsOpen(true),
    close: () => setIsOpen(false),
  };
};
```

And then use this hook in our `App` instead of setting state directly:

```
const App = () => {
  // state is in the hook now
  const { isOpen, open, close } = useModalDialog();
```

```
  return (
    <div className="layout">
      {/* just use "open" method from the hook */}
      <Button onClick={open}>Open dialog</Button>
      {/* just use "close" method from the hook */}
      {isOpen ? <ModalDialog onClose={close} /> : null}
      <VerySlowComponent />
      <BunchOfStuff />
      <OtherStuffAlsoComplicated />
    </div>
  );
};
```

Why did I call this "the danger"? It seems like a reasonable pattern, and the
code is slightly cleaner. Because the hook hides the fact that we have state
in the app. But the state is still there! Every time it changes, it will still
trigger a re-render of the component that uses this hook. It doesn't even
matter whether this state is used in the App directly or even whether the
hook returns anything.

Interactive example and full code
https://advanced-react.com/examples/01/04

If, for example, I want to be fancy with this dialog's positioning and
introduce some state inside that hook that listens for the window's resize:

```
const useModalDialog = () => {
  const [width, setWidth] = useState(0);

  useEffect(() => {
    const listener = () => {
      setWidth(window.innerWidth);
    }

    window.addEventListener('resize', listener);

    return () => window.removeEventListener('resize', listener);
  }, []);
```

```
// return is the same
return ...
}
```

The entire `App` component will re-render on every resize, even though this value is not even returned from the hook!

Interactive example and full code
https://advanced-react.com/examples/01/05

Hooks are essentially just pockets in your trousers. If, instead of carrying a 10-kilogram dumbbell in your hands, you put it in your pocket, it wouldn't change the fact that it's still hard to run: you have 10 kilograms of additional weight on your person. But if you put that ten kilograms in a self-driving trolley, you can run around freely and fresh and maybe even stop for coffee: the trolley will take care of itself. Components for the state are that trolley.

Exactly the same logic applies to the hooks that use other hooks: *anything* that can trigger a re-render, however deep in the chain of hooks it's happening, will trigger a re-render in the component that uses that very first hook. If I extract that additional state into a hook that returns `null`, `App` will still re-render on every resize:

```
const useResizeDetector = () => {
  const [width, setWidth] = useState(0);

  useEffect(() => {
    const listener = () => {
      setWidth(window.innerWidth);
    };

    window.addEventListener('resize', listener);

    return () => window.removeEventListener('resize', listener);
  }, []);
```

```
    return null;
  }

  const useModalDialog = () => {
    // I don't even use it, just call it here
    useResizeDetector();

    // return is the same
    return ...
  }

  const App = () => {
    // this hook uses useResizeDetector underneath that triggers state
  update on resize
    // the entire App will re-render on every resize!
    const { isOpen, open, close } = useModalDialog();

    return // same return
  }
```

Interactive example and full code
https://advanced-react.com/examples/01/06

So, be careful with those.

In order to fix our app, you'd still need to extract that button, dialog, and the custom hook into a component:

```
  const ButtonWithModalDialog = () => {
    const { isOpen, open, close } = useModalDialog();

    // render only Button and ModalDialog here
    return (
      <>
        <Button onClick={open}>Open dialog</Button>
        {isOpen ? <ModalDialog onClose={close} /> : null}
      </>
    );
  };
```

So, where you put state is very important. Ideally, to avoid future performance problems, you'd want to isolate it as much as possible to as tiny and light components as possible. In the next chapter (*Chapter 2. Elements, children as props, and re-renders*), we'll take a look at another pattern that helps with exactly that.

Key takeaways

This is just the beginning. In the following chapters, we'll dig into more details on how all of this works. In the meantime, here are some key points to remember from this Chapter:

- Re-rendering is how React updates components with new data. Without re-renders, there will be no interactivity in our apps.
- State update is the initial source of all re-renders.
- If a component's re-render is triggered, all nested components inside that component will be re-rendered.
- During the normal React re-renders cycle (without the use of memoization), props change doesn't matter: components will re-render even if they don't have any props.
- We can use the pattern known as "moving state down" to prevent unnecessary re-renders in big apps.
- State update in a hook will trigger the re-render of a component that uses this hook, even if the state itself is not used.
- In the case of hooks using other hooks, any state update within that chain of hooks will trigger the re-render of a component that uses the very first hook.

Chapter 2. Elements, children as props, and re-renders

In the previous chapter, we explored how state changes trigger downstream re-renders in our apps and how this can be dealt with using the "moving state down" pattern. However, the example there was relatively simple, and the state was pretty isolated. So moving it into a component was easy. What are our options when the situation is a bit more complicated?

It's time to continue our exploration of how re-renders work, do another performance investigation, and dig deeper into the details. In this chapter, you'll learn:

- How passing components as props can improve the performance of our apps.
- How exactly React triggers re-renders.
- Why components as props are not affected by re-renders.
- What an Element is, how it's different from a Component, and why it's important to know that distinction.
- The basics of React reconciliation and diffing.
- What the "children as props" pattern is, and how it can prevent re-renders.

The problem

Imagine again that you've inherited a large, complicated, and very performance-sensitive app. And that app has a scrollable content area. Probably some fancy layout with a sticky header, a collapsible sidebar on the left, and the rest of the functionality in the middle.

The code for that main scrollable area looks something like this:

```
const App = () => {
  return (
    <div className="scrollable-block">
      <VerySlowComponent />
      <BunchOfStuff />
      <OtherStuffAlsoComplicated />
    </div>
  );
};
```

Just a div with a `className` and CSS `overflow: auto` underneath.
And lots of very slow components inside that div. On your very first day on
the job, you're asked to implement a very creative feature: a block that
shows up at the bottom of the area when a user scrolls for a bit and slowly
moves to the top as the user continues to scroll down. Or slowly moves
down and disappears if the user scrolls up. Something like a secondary
navigation block with some useful links. And, of course, the scrolling and
everything associated with it should be smooth and lag-free.

The simplest way to implement these requirements would be to attach an
`onScroll` handler to the scrollable div, capture the scrolled value, and
calculate the position of the floating div based on that:

```
const MainScrollableArea = () => {
  const [position, setPosition] = useState(300);

  const onScroll = (e) => {
    // calculate position based on the scrolled value
    const calculated = getPosition(e.target.scrollTop);
    // save it to state
    setPosition(calculated);
  };

  return (
    <div className="scrollable-block" onScroll={onScroll}>
      {/* pass position value to the new movable component */}
      <MovingBlock position={position} />
      <VerySlowComponent />
      <BunchOfStuff />
```

```
      <OtherStuffAlsoComplicated />
    </div>
  );
};
```

Interactive example and full code
https://advanced-react.com/examples/02/01

However, from the performance and re-renders perspective, this is far from optimal. Every scroll will trigger a state update, and as we already know, the state update will trigger a re-render of the `App` component and every nested component inside. So all the very slow bunch of stuff will re-render, and the scrolling experience will be slow and laggy. Exactly the opposite of what we need.

And as you can see, we can't just easily extract that state into a component anymore. The `setPosition` is used in the `onScroll` function, which is attached to the div that wraps everything.

So, what to do here? Memoization or some magic with passing Ref around? Not necessarily! As before, there's a simpler option. We can still extract that state and everything needed for the state to work into a component:

```
const ScrollableWithMovingBlock = () => {
  const [position, setPosition] = useState(300);

  const onScroll = (e) => {
    const calculated = getPosition(e.target.scrollTop);
    setPosition(calculated);
  };

  return (
    <div className="scrollable-block" onScroll={onScroll}>
      <MovingBlock position={position} />
      {/* slow bunch of stuff used to be here, but not anymore */}
    </div>
  );
};
```

And then just pass that slow bunch of stuff to that component as props. Something like this:

```
const App = () => {
  const slowComponents = (
    <>
      <VerySlowComponent />
      <BunchOfStuff />
      <OtherStuffAlsoComplicated />
    </>
  );

  return (
    <ScrollableWithMovingBlock content={slowComponents} />
  );
};
```

Just create a "content" property in our `ScrollableWithMovingBlock` component that accepts React Elements (more details about those a bit later). And then, inside `ScrollableWithMovingBlock`, accept that prop and put it where it was supposed to render:

```
// add "content" property to the component
const ScrollableWithMovingBlock = ({ content }) => {
  const [position, setPosition] = useState(0);
  const onScroll = () => {...} // same as before

  return (
    <div className="scrollable-block" onScroll={onScroll}>
      <MovingBlock position={position} />
      {content}
    </div>
  )
}
```

Now, onto the state update and re-renders situation. If a state update is triggered, we will once again trigger a re-render of a component, as usual. However, in this case, it will be the `ScrollableWithMovingBlock` component - just a div with a movable block. The rest of the slow components are passed through props, they are *outside* of that component. In the "hierarchical" components tree, they belong to the parent. And remember? React never goes "up" that tree when it re-renders a component. So our slow components won't re-render when the state is updated, and the scrolling experience will be smooth and lag-free.

Interactive example and full code
https://advanced-react.com/examples/02/02

Wait a second, some might think here. This doesn't make much sense. Yes, those components are declared in the parent, but they are still rendered *inside* that component with the state. So why don't they re-render? It's actually a very reasonable question.

To make sense of all of this, we need to understand a few things: what we actually mean by "re-render" in React, what the difference is between an Element and a Component, and the basics of the reconciliation and diffing algorithms.

Elements, Components, and re-renders

First of all, a Component - what is it? Here's the simplest one:

```
const Parent = () => {
  return <Child />;
};
```

As you can see, it's just a function. What makes a component different from any other function is that it returns Elements, which React then converts into DOM elements and sends to the browser to be drawn on the screen. If it has props, those would be just the first argument of that function:

```
const Parent = (props) => {
  return <Child />;
};
```

This function returns `<Child />` , which is an Element of a `Child` Component. Every time we use those brackets on a component, we create an Element. The Element of the `Parent` component would be `<Parent />` .

An Element is simply an object that *defines* a component that needs to be rendered on the screen. In fact, the nice HTML-like syntax is nothing more than syntax sugar for the `React.createElement` function[1]. We can even replace that element with this: `React.createElement(Child, null, null)` and everything will work as expected.

The object definition for our `<Child />` element would look something like this:

```
{
  type: Child,
  props: {}, // if Child had props
  ... // lots of other internal React stuff
}
```

This tells us that the `Parent` component, which returns that definition, wants us to render the `Child` component with no props. The return of the `Child` component will have its own definitions, and so on, until we reach the end of that chain of components.

Elements are not limited to components; they can be just normal DOM elements. Our `Child` could return an `h1` tag, for example:

```
const Child = () => {
  return <h1>Some title</h1>;
};
```

In this case, the definition object will be exactly the same and behave the same, only the type will be a string:

```
{
  type: "h1",
  ... // props and internal react stuff
}
```

Now to re-render. What we usually refer to as "re-render" is React calling those functions and executing everything that needs to be executed in the process (like hooks). From the return of those functions, React builds a tree of those objects. We know it as the Fiber Tree now, or Virtual DOM sometimes. In fact, it's even two trees: before and after re-render. By comparing ("diffing") those, React will then extract information that goes to the browser: which DOM elements need to be updated, removed, or added. This is known as the "reconciliation" algorithm.

The part that matters for this chapter's problem is this: if the object (Element) before and after re-render is exactly the same, then React will skip the re-render of the Component this Element represents and its nested components. And by "exactly the same," I mean whether `Object.is(ElementBeforeRerender, ElementAfterRerender)` returns `true`. React doesn't perform the deep comparison of objects. If the result of this comparison is `true`, then React will leave that component in peace and move on to the next one.

If the comparison returns `false`, this is the signal to React that something has changed. It will look at the `type` then. If the `type` is the same, then React will re-render this component. If the `type` changes, then it will remove the "old" component and mount the "new" one. We'll take a look at it in more detail in *Chapter 6. Deep dive into diffing and reconciliation.*

Let's take a look at the Parent/Child example again and imagine our `Parent` has state:

```
const Parent = (props) => {
  const [state, setState] = useState();

  return <Child />;
};
```

When `setState` is called, React will know to re-render the `Parent` component. So it will call the `Parent` function and compare whatever it returns before and after state changes. And it returns an object that is defined *locally* to the `Parent` function. So on every function call (i.e. re-render), this object will be re-created, and the result of `Object.is` on "before" and "after" `<Child />` objects will be `false`. As a result, every time the `Parent` here re-renders, the `Child` will also re-render. Which we already know, but it's nice to have proof of this, isn't it?

Now, imagine what will happen here if, instead of rendering that `Child` component directly, I would pass it as a prop?

```
const Parent = ({ child }) => {
  const [state, setState] = useState();

  return child;
};

// someone somewhere renders Parent component like this
<Parent child={<Child />} />;
```

Somewhere, where the `Parent` component is rendered, the `<Child />` definition object is created and passed to it as the `child` prop. When the state update in `Parent` is triggered, React will compare what the `Parent` function returns "before" and "after" state change. And in this case, it will be a reference to the `child`: an object that is created *outside* of the `Parent` function scope and therefore doesn't change when it's called. As a result, the comparison of `child` "before" and "after" will return `true`, and React will skip the re-render of this component.

And this is exactly what we did for our component with the scroll!

```
const ScrollableWithMovingBlock = ({ content }) => {
  const [position, setPosition] = useState(300);
  const onScroll = () => {...} // same as before

  return (
    <div className="scrollable-block" onScroll={onScroll}>
```

```
    <MovingBlock position={position} />
    {content}
  </div>
)
}
```

When `setPosition` in `ScrollableWithMovingBlock` is triggered, and re-render happens, React will compare all those object definitions that the function returns, will see that the `content` object is exactly the same before and after, and will skip the re-render of whatever is there. In our case - a bunch of very slow components.

`<MovingBlock ... />`, however, will re-render: it's created inside `ScrollableWithMovingBlock`. The object will be re-created on every re-render, and the comparison "before" and "after" will return `false`.

Children as props

While this pattern is cool and totally valid, there is one small problem with it: it looks weird. Passing the entire page content into some random props just feels... wrong for some reason. So, let's improve it.

First of all, let's talk about the nature of props. Props are just an object that we pass as the first argument to our component function. Everything that we extract from it is a prop. *Everything.* In our Parent/Child code, if I rename the `child` prop to `children`, nothing will change: it will continue to work.

```
// before
const Parent = ({ child }) => {
  return child;
};

// after
const Parent = ({ children }) => {
  return children;
};
```

And on the consumer side, the same situation: nothing changes.

```
// before
<Parent child={<Child />} />

// after
<Parent children={<Child />} />
```

However, for `children` props, we have a special syntax in `JSX`. That nice nesting composition that we use all the time with `HTML` tags, we just never thought about it and paid attention to it:

```
<Parent>
  <Child />
</Parent>
```

This will work exactly the same way as if we were passing the `children` prop explicitly:

```
<Parent children={<Child />} />

// exactly the same as above
<Parent>
  <Child />
</Parent>
```

And will be represented as this object:

```
{
  type: Parent,
  props: {
    // element for Child here
    children: {
      type: Child,
      ...
    },
  }
}
```

And it will have exactly the same performance benefits as passing Elements as props as well! Whatever is passed through props won't be affected by the state change of the component that receives those props. So we can re-write our `App` from this:

```
const App = () => {
  const slowComponents = (
    <>
      <VerySlowComponent />
      <BunchOfStuff />
      <OtherStuffAlsoComplicated />
    </>
  );

  return (
    <ScrollableWithMovingBlock content={slowComponents} />
  );
};
```

To something much prettier and easier to understand:

```
const App = () => {
  return (
    <ScrollableWithMovingBlock>
      <VerySlowComponent />
      <BunchOfStuff />
      <OtherStuffAlsoComplicated />
    </ScrollableWithMovingBlock>
  );
};
```

All we need to do in the `ScrollableWithMovingBlock` component is to rename the `content` prop to `children`, nothing else! Before:

```
const ScrollableWithMovingBlock = ({ content }) => {
  // .. the rest of the code

  return (
    <div ...>
```

```
      ...
      {content}
    </div>
  )
}
```

After:

```
const ScrollableWithMovingBlock = ({ children }) => {
  // .. the rest of the code

  return (
    <div ...>
      ...
      {children}
    </div>
  )
}
```

And here we go: implemented a very performant scrollable block in a very slow app using just a small composition trick.

> **Interactive example and full code**
> https://advanced-react.com/examples/02/03

Key takeaways

Hope this made sense and you're now confident with the "components as props" and "children as props" patterns. In the next chapter, we'll take a look at how components as props can be useful outside of performance. In the meantime, here are a few things to remember:

- A Component is just a function that accepts an argument (props) and returns Elements that should be rendered when this Component renders on the screen. `const A = () => <B />` is a Component.

- An Element is an object that describes what needs to be rendered on the screen, with the type either a string for DOM elements or a reference to a Component for components. `const b = <B />` is an Element.
- Re-render is just React calling the Component's function.
- A component re-renders when its element object changes, as determined by `Object.is` comparison of it before and after re-render.
- When elements are passed as props to a component, and this component triggers a re-render through a state update, elements that are passed as props won't re-render.
- "children" are just props and behave like any other prop when they are passed via `JSX` nesting syntax:

```
<Parent>
  <Child />
</Parent>

// the same as:
<Parent children={<Child />} />
```

Chapter 3. Configuration concerns with elements as props

In the previous chapter, we explored how passing elements as props can improve the performance of our apps. However, performance enhancements are not the most common use of this pattern. In fact, they are more of a nice side effect and relatively unknown. The biggest use case this pattern solves is actually flexibility and configuration of components.

Let's continue our investigation into how React works. This time, we're going to build a simple "button with icon" component. What could possibly be complicated about this one, right? But in the process of building it, you'll find out:

- How elements as props can drastically improve configuration concerns for such components.
- How conditional rendering of components influences performance.
- When a component passed as props is rendered *exactly*.
- How to set default props for components passed as props by using the `cloneElement` function, and what the downsides of that are.

Ready? Let's go!

The problem

Imagine, for example, that you need to implement a `Button` component. One of the requirements is that the button should be able to show the "loading" icon on the right when it's used in the "loading" context. Quite a common pattern for data sending in forms.

No problem! We can just implement the button and add the `isLoading` prop, based on which we'll render the icon.

```
const Button = ({ isLoading }) => {
  return (
    <button>Submit {isLoading ? <Loading /> : null}</button>
  );
};
```

The next day, this button needs to support all available icons from your
library, not only the `Loading`. Okay, we can add the `iconName` prop to
the `Button` for that. The next day - people want to be able to control the
color of that icon so that it aligns better with the color palette used on the
website. The `iconColor` prop is added. Then `iconSize`, to control the
size of the icon. And then, a use case appears for the button to support icons
on the left side as well. And avatars.

Eventually, half of the props on the `Button` are there just to control those
icons, no one is able to understand what is happening inside, and every
change results in some broken functionality for the customers.

```
const Button = ({
  isLoading,
  iconLeftName,
  iconLeftColor,
  iconLeftSize,
  isIconLeftAvatar,
  ...
}) => {
  // no one knows what's happening here and how all those props work
  return ...
}
```

Sounds familiar?

Elements as props

Luckily, there is an easy way to drastically improve this situation. All we
need to do is to get rid of those configuration props and pass the icon as an
Element instead:

```
const Button = ({ icon }) => {
  return <button>Submit {icon}</button>;
};
```

And then leave it to the consumer to configure that icon in whatever way they want:

```
// default Loading icon
<Button icon={<Loading />} />

// red Error icon
<Button icon={<Error color="red" />} />

// yellow large Warning icon
<Button icon={<Warning color="yellow" size="large" />} />

// avatar instead of icon
<Button icon={<Avatar />} />
```

Interactive example and full code
https://advanced-react.com/examples/03/01

Whether doing something like this for a `Button` is a good idea or not is sometimes debatable, of course. It highly depends on how strict your design is and how much deviation it allows for those who implement product features.

But imagine implementing something like a modal dialog with a header, content area, and footer with some buttons.

Unless your designers are *very* strict and powerful, chances are you'd need to have different configurations of those buttons in different dialogs: one, two, three buttons, one button is a link, one button is "primary," different texts on those of course, different icons, different tooltips, etc. Imagine passing all of that through configuration props!

But with elements as props, it couldn't be easier: just create a `footer` prop on the dialog

```
const ModalDialog = ({ content, footer }) => {
  return (
    <div className="modal-dialog">
      <div className="content">{content}</div>
      <div className="footer">{footer}</div>
    </div>
  );
};
```

and then pass whatever is needed:

```
// just one button in footer
<ModalDialog content={<SomeFormHere />} footer={<SubmitButton />} />

// two buttons
<ModalDialog
  content={<SomeFormHere />}
  footer={<><SubmitButton /><CancelButton /></>}
/>
```

Interactive example and full code
https://advanced-react.com/examples/03/02

Or something like a `ThreeColumnsLayout` component, which renders three columns with some content on the screen. In this case, you can't even do any configuration: it literally can and should render *anything* in those columns.

```
<ThreeColumnsLayout
  leftColumn={<Something />}
  middleColumn={<OtherThing />}
  rightColumn={<SomethingElse />}
/>
```

Essentially, an element as a prop for a component is a way to tell the consumer: give me whatever you want, I don't know or care what it is, I am just responsible for putting it in the right place. The rest is up to you.

And, of course, the "children" as props pattern, described in the previous chapter, is very useful here as well. If we want to pass something that we consider a "main" part of that component, like the "content" area in the modal dialog, or the middle column in the three columns layout, we can just use the nested syntax for that:

```
// before
<ModalDialog
  content={<SomeFormHere />}
  footer={<SubmitButton />}
/>

// after
<ModalDialog
  footer={<SubmitButton />}
>
  <SomeFormHere />
</ModalDialog>
```

All we need to do, from the `ModalDialog` perspective, is to rename the "content" prop to "children":

```
const ModalDialog = ({ children, footer }) => {
  return (
    <div className="dialog">
      <div className="content">{children}</div>
      <div className="footer">{footer}</div>
    </div>
  );
};
```

Always remember: "children" in this context are nothing more than a prop, and the "nested" syntax is just syntax sugar for it!

Conditional rendering and performance

One of the biggest concerns that sometimes arises with this pattern is the performance of it. Which is ironic, considering that in the previous chapter, we discussed how to use it to improve performance. So, what's going on?

Imagine we render the component that accepts elements as props conditionally. Like our `ModalDialog` , that typically would be rendered only when the `isDialogOpen` variable is true:

```
const App = () => {
  const [isDialogOpen, setIsDialogOpen] = useState(false);

  // when is this one going to be rendered?
  const footer = <Footer />;

  return isDialogOpen ? (
    <ModalDialog footer={footer} />
  ) : null;
};
```

The question here, with which even very experienced developers sometimes struggle, is this: we declare our `Footer` *before* the dialog. While the dialog is still closed and won't be open for a while (or maybe never). Does this mean that the footer *will always be rendered*, even if the dialog is not on the screen? What about the performance implications? Won't this slow down the `App` component?

Fortunately, we have nothing to worry about here. Remember, how in *Chapter 2. Elements, children as props, and re-renders* we discussed what an Element is? All we did when we declared the `footer` variable (`footer = <Footer />`) was create an Element, nothing more. From the React and code perspective, it's just an object that sits in memory quietly and does nothing. And creating objects is cheap (at least compared to rendering components).

This `Footer` will actually be rendered *only* when it ends up in the return object of one of the components, not sooner. In our case, it will be the `ModalDialog` component. It doesn't matter that the `<Footer />` element was created in the `App`. It's the `ModalDialog` that will take it and actually return it:

```
const ModalDialog = ({ children, footer }) => {
  return (
    <div className="dialog">
      <div className="content">{children}</div>
      {/* Whatever is coming from footer prop is going to be rendered
only when this entire component renders */}
      {/* not sooner */}
      <div className="footer">{footer}</div>
    </div>
  );
};
```

This is what makes routing patterns, like in one of the versions of React router, completely safe:

```
const App = () => {
  return (
    <>
      <Route path="/some/path" element={<Page />} />
      <Route path="/other/path" element={<OtherPage />} />
      ...
    </>
  );
};
```

There is no condition here, so it *feels* like the `App` owns and renders both `<Page />` and `<OtherPage />` at the same time. But it doesn't. It just creates small objects that *describe* those pages. The actual rendering will only happen when the `path` in one of the routes matches the URL and the `element` prop is actually returned from the `Route` component.

Default values for the elements from props

Let's talk about our button and its icons a little bit more.

One of the objections against passing those icons as props is that this pattern is *too* flexible. It's okay for the `ThreeColumnsLayout` component to accept anything in the `leftColumn` prop. But in the Button's case, we don't really want to pass *everything* there. In the real world, the `Button` would need to have some degree of control over the icons. If the button has the `isDisabled` property, you'd likely want the icon to appear "disabled" as well. Bigger buttons would want bigger icons by default. Blue buttons would want white icons by default, and white buttons would want black icons.

However, if we leave the implementation as it is now, this will be problematic: it will be up to the `Button` 's consumers to remember all that.

```jsx
// primary button should have white icons
<Button appearance="primary" icon={<Loading color="white" />} />

// secondary button should have black icons
<Button appearance="secondary" icon={<Loading color="black" />} />

// large button should have large icons
<Button size="large" icon={<Loading size="large" />} />
```

Half of the time, it will be forgotten, and the other half misunderstood. What we need here is to assign some default values to those icons that the

`Button` can control while still preserving the flexibility of the pattern.

Luckily, we can do exactly that. Remember that these icons in props are just objects with known and predictable shapes. And React has APIs that allow us to operate on them easily. In our case, we can clone the icon in the `Button` with the help of the `React.cloneElement` function[2], and assign any props to that new element that we want. So nothing stops us from creating some default icon props, merging them together with the props coming from the original icon, and assigning them to the cloned icon:

```
const Button = ({ appearance, size, icon }) => {
  // create default props
  const defaultIconProps = {
    size: size === 'large' ? 'large' : 'medium',
    color: appearance === 'primary' ? 'white' : 'black',
  };
  const newProps = {
    ...defaultIconProps,
    // make sure that props that are coming from the icon override
default if they exist
    ...icon.props,
  };
  // clone the icon and assign new props to it
  const clonedIcon = React.cloneElement(icon, newProps);

  return <button>Submit {clonedIcon}</button>;
};
```

And now, all of our `Button` with icon examples will be reduced to just this:

```
// primary button will have white icons
<Button appearance="primary" icon={<Loading />} />

// secondary button will have black icons
<Button appearance="secondary" icon={<Loading />} />

// large button will have large icons
<Button size="large" icon={<Loading />} />
```

No additional props on any of the icons, just the default props that are controlled by the button now! And then, if someone *really* needs to override the default value, they can still do it: by passing the prop as usual.

```
// override the default black color with red icons
<Button
  appearance="secondary"
  icon={<Loading color="red" />}
/>
```

In fact, consumers of the `Button` won't even know about the default props. For them, the icon will just work like magic.

Why we shouldn't go crazy with default values

Speaking of magic: the fact that setting default values works seemingly magically can be a big downside. The biggest problem here is that it's way too easy to make a mistake and override the props for good. If, for example, I don't override the default props with the actual props and just assign them right away:

```
const Button = ({ appearance, size, icon }) => {
  // create default props
  const defaultIconProps = {
    size: size === 'large' ? 'large' : 'medium',
    color: appearance === 'primary' ? 'white' : 'black',
  };

  // clone the icon and assign the default props to it - don't do
that!
  // it will override all the props that are passed to the icon from
the outside!
  const clonedIcon = React.cloneElement(
    icon,
    defaultIconProps,
```

Page 47

```
  );

  return <button>Submit {clonedIcon}</button>;
};
```

I will basically destroy the icon's API. People will try to pass different sizes
or colors to it, but it will never reach the target:

```
// color "red" won't work here - I never passed those props to the
cloned icon
<Button appearance="secondary" icon={<Loading color="red" />} />

// but if I just render this icon outside the button, it will work
<Loading color="red" />
```

Interactive example and full code
https://advanced-react.com/examples/03/06

Good luck to anyone trying to understand why setting the color of the icon
outside of the button works perfectly, but doesn't work if the icon is passed
as this prop.

So be very careful with this pattern, and make sure you always override the
default props with the actual props. And if you feel uneasy about it - no
worries. In React, there are a million ways to achieve exactly the same
result. There is another pattern that can be very helpful for this case: render
props. It can also be very helpful if you need to calculate the icon's props
based on the button's state or just plainly pass that state back to the icon.
The next chapter is all about this pattern.

Key takeaways

Before we move on to the Render Props pattern, let's remember:

- When a component renders another component, the configuration of which is controlled by props, we can pass the entire component element as a prop instead, leaving the configuration concerns to the consumer.

```
const Button = ({ icon }) => {
  return <button>Submit {icon}</button>;
};

// large red Error icon
<Button icon={<Error color="red" size="large" />} />;
```

- If a component that has elements as props is rendered conditionally, then even if those elements are created outside of the condition, they will only be rendered when the conditional component is rendered.

```
const App = () => {
  // footer will be rendered only when the dialog itself renders
  // after isDialogOpen is set to "true"
  const footer = <Footer />;

  return isDialogOpen ? (
    <ModalDialog footer={footer} />
  ) : null;
};
```

- If we need to provide default props to the element from props, we can use the `cloneElement` function for that.
- This pattern, however, is very fragile. It's too easy to make a mistake there, so use it only for very simple cases.

Chapter 4. Advanced configuration with render props

In the previous chapter, we talked about flexibility, component configuration, how to pass elements as props to solve that, and how to set default values on those. But elements as props, however great they are, don't solve everything for us. If a component that accepts other components through props needs to influence their props or pass some state to them in some explicit non-magical way, then elements as props and the `cloneElement` function are no help here.

This is where the pattern known as "render props" comes in handy. In this chapter, you'll learn:

- What the render props pattern is and what kind of configuration concerns it solves, but elements as props can't.
- How to share stateful logic with render props and how children as render props look like.
- Why we shouldn't actually do that these days, now that we have hooks.
- When the render props for sharing logic pattern can still be useful, even in the hooks era.

The problem

Here is the `Button` component that we implemented in the previous chapter:

```
const Button = ({ appearance, size, icon }) => {
  // create default props
  const defaultIconProps = {
    size: size === 'large' ? 'large' : 'medium',
```

```
    color: appearance === 'primary' ? 'white' : 'black',
  };
  const newProps = {
    ...defaultIconProps,
    // make sure that props that are coming from the icon override
  default if they exist
    ...icon.props,
  };

  // clone the icon and assign new props to it
  const clonedIcon = React.cloneElement(icon, newProps);

  return (
    <button className={`button ${appearance}`}>
      Submit {clonedIcon}
    </button>
  );
};
```

The `Button` accepts an `icon` Element and sets its `size` and `color`
props by default.

While this approach works pretty well for simple cases, it is not that good
for something more complicated. What if I want to introduce some state to
the `Button` and give `Button`'s consumers access to that state? Like
adjusting the icon while the button is hovered, for example? It's easy
enough to implement that state in the button:

```
const Button = ({ ... }) => {
  const [isHovered, setIsHovered] = useState();

  return <button onMouseOver={() => setIsHovered(true)} />
}
```

But then what? How do we share it with the icon?

Another problem with this approach is that we're making some major
assumptions about the Element that comes through the `icon` prop. We
expect it to have at least `size` and `color` props. What if we wanted to
use a different library for icons, and those icons didn't have those exact

props? Our default props logic will just stop working with no way of fixing it.

Render props for rendering Elements

Luckily, as I mentioned before, there are one million ways to solve exactly the same problem in React. In this case, instead of passing elements as a prop, we can pass them as a *render prop* (or *render function*). A render prop is nothing more than just a function that returns an Element. That function is almost the same as a Component. Only a Component you wouldn't call directly - React does it for you. But a render function is under your command.

In the case of the `Button` and its icon, here is how it would look like with the render function:

```
// instead of "icon" that expects an Element
// we're receiving a function that returns an Element
const Button = ({ renderIcon }) => {
  // and then just calling this function where the icon should be
rendered
  return <button>Submit {renderIcon()}</button>;
};
```

We accept a `renderIcon` function and just call it where the icon is supposed to go. And then, on the consumer side, we'd pass the function that returns the icon instead of passing the icon directly:

```
<Button renderIcon={() => <HomeIcon />} />
```

And we can still adjust that icon to our needs, of course, same as the regular Element:

```
// red icon
<Button renderIcon={() => <HomeIcon color="red" /> } />
```

```
// large icon
<Button renderIcon={() => <HomeIcon size="large" /> } />
```

So, what's the point of using this function? First of all, icons' props. Now, instead of cloning elements, which is a bit of a shady move anyway, we can just pass the object to the function:

```
const Button = ({ appearance, size, renderIcon }) => {
  // create default props as before
  const defaultIconProps = {
    size: size === 'large' ? 'large' : 'medium',
    color: appearance === 'primary' ? 'white' : 'black',
  };

  // and just pass them to the function
  return (
    <button>Submit {renderIcon(defaultIconProps)}</button>
  );
};
```

And then, on the icon's side, we can accept them and spread them over the icon:

```
<Button renderIcon={(props) => <HomeIcon {...props} />} />
```

We can override some of them:

```
<Button
  renderIcon={(props) => (
    <HomeIcon {...props} size="large" color="red" />
  )}
/>
```

Or convert them to the props our icon actually accepts:

```
<Button
  renderIcon={(props) => (
    <HomeIcon
```

```
      fontSize={props.size}
      style={{ color: props.color }}
    />
  )}
/>
```

Interactive example and full code
https://advanced-react.com/examples/04/01

Everything is explicit, and nothing overrides anything by some hidden magic. The flow of data, although a bit loopy, is visible and traceable.

```
<Button renderIcon={(props) => <Icon {...props}/>}>…</Button>

const Button = ({ renderIcon }) => {
  return (
    <button>
      {renderIcon({ color: "green" })}
    </button>
  )
}
```

Sharing state is also not a problem anymore. We can simply merge that state value into the object we're passing to the icon:

```
const Button = ({ appearance, size, renderIcon }) => {
  const [isHovered, setIsHovered] = useState(false);

  const iconParams = {
    size: size === 'large' ? 'large' : 'medium',
    color: appearance === 'primary' ? 'white' : 'black',
    // add state here – it's just an object after all
    isHovered,
  }
```

```
  return <button ...>Submit {renderIcon(iconParams)}</button>
}
```

Or we can even go fancy and pass it as a second argument to clearly separate state and props. Whatever makes sense for our codebase:

```
const Button = ({ appearance, size, renderIcon }) => {
  const [isHovered, setIsHovered] = useState(false);

  const iconParams = {
    size: size === 'large' ? 'large' : 'medium',
    color: appearance === 'primary' ? 'white' : 'black',
  }

  // pass state here as a second argument
  return <button ...>Submit {renderIcon(iconParams, { isHovered })}
</button>
}
```

And then on the icon side, we can again do whatever we want with that hovered state. We can render another icon:

```
const icon = (props, state) => state.isHovered ? <HomeIconHovered
{...props} /> : <HomeIcon {...props} />

<Button renderIcon={icon} />
```

Apply a different className:

```
const icon = (props, state) => <HomeIcon {...props} className=
{state.isHovered ? 'hovered' : ''} />

<Button renderIcon={icon} />
```

Or just ignore it completely.

Interactive example and full code
https://advanced-react.com/examples/04/02

Sharing stateful logic: children as render props

Another useful application for render props is sharing stateful logic between components, and it usually goes in combination with the "children as props" pattern. As discussed in the previous chapter, "children," when used as HTML-like nested syntax, are nothing more than a prop:

```
<Parent>
  <Child />
</Parent>

// exactly the same as above
<Parent children={<Child />} />
```

So nothing actually stops us from making `children` a function as well. We don't even have to prefix it with `render`. `renderSomething` is just a naming convention. It would look like this:

```
// make it a function
<Parent children={() => <Child />} />
```

And in `Parent`, you'd call it like any other render prop:

```
const Parent = ({ children }) => {
  // it's just a function that returns an element, just call it here
  return children();
};
```

The pretty nested syntax will work with this as well:

```
<Parent>{() => <Child />}</Parent>
```

Why can it be useful? Imagine, for example, you're implementing a "resize detector" component. A component that tracks the resize event on the browser window:

```
const ResizeDetector = () => {
  const [width, setWidth] = useState();

  useEffect(() => {
    const listener = () => {
      const width = window.innerWidth;
      setWidth(width)
    }
    window.addEventListener("resize", listener);
    // the rest of the code
  }, [])

  return ...
}
```

And you want to make it generic so that different components throughout the app can track the window width without implementing that code everywhere. So `ResizeDetector` needs to share that state with other components somehow. Technically, we could do this through props, just by adding the `onWidthChange` prop to the detector:

```
const ResizeDetector = ({ onWidthChange }) => {
  const [width, setWidth] = useState();

  useEffect(() => {
    const listener = () => {
      const width = window.innerWidth;
      setWidth(width);
      // trigger onWidthChange prop here
      onWidthChange(width);
    }
```

```
    window.addEventListener("resize", listener);
    // the rest of the code
  }, [])

  return ...
}
```

But this would mean that any component that wants to use it would have to
maintain its own state for it:

```
const Layout = () => {
  const [windowWidth, setWindowWidth] = useState(0);

  return (
    <>
      <ResizeDetector onWindowWidth={setWindowWidth} />
      {windowWidth > 600 ? (
        <WideLayout />
      ) : (
        <NarrowLayout />
      )}
    </>
  );
};
```

A bit messy.

What we can do instead is just make `ResizeDetector` accept
`children` as a function and pass that `width` to children directly:

```
const ResizeDetector = ({ children }) => {
  const [width, setWidth] = useState();

  // same code as before

  // pass width to children
  return children(width);
};
```

Then, any component that needs that width can just use it without introducing unnecessary state for it:

```
const Layout = () => {
  return (
    <ResizeDetector>
      {(windowWidth) => {
        // no more state! Get it directly from the resizer
        return windowWidth > 600 ? (
          <WideLayout />
        ) : (
          <NarrowLayout />
        );
      }}
    </ResizeDetector>
  );
};
```

Interactive example and full code
https://advanced-react.com/examples/04/04

In real life, of course, we'd have a re-renders problem here: we're triggering state updates on every width change. So we'd have to either calculate the layout inside the detector or debounce it. But the principle of sharing state will remain the same.

Also, in modern code, we probably wouldn't use this at all because...

Hooks replaced render props

Anyone who's done any coding in React in the last two years is probably thinking something like this right now: "Hey, what you're saying doesn't make sense. Why do you do something as complicated as this when we have hooks for sharing stateful logic?"

And you're absolutely right! Hooks replaced that pattern in almost 99% of cases. And rightfully so. Exactly the same use case can be rewritten with hooks like this:

```
const useResizeDetector = () => {
  const [width, setWidth] = useState();

  useEffect(() => {
    const listener = () => {
      const width = ... // get window width here
      setWidth(width);
    }
    window.addEventListener("resize", listener);
    // the rest of the code
  }, [])

  return width;
}
```

Just extract the entire logic of the `ResizeDetector` component into a hook and then use it everywhere:

```
const Layout = () => {
  const windowWidth = useResizeDetector();

  return windowWidth > 600 ? (
    <WideLayout />
  ) : (
    <NarrowLayout />
  );
};
```

Interactive example and full code
https://advanced-react.com/examples/04/05

Less code, and much easier to understand what's going on.

So why learn this pattern at all? A few reasons for this:

- Render props for configuration and flexibility use cases, described at the beginning, are still very viable.
- If you are working on a project that is a few years old, this pattern will be all over the codebase. It was *really* popular before the introduction of hooks, especially for encapsulating form validation logic. A few popular libraries still use it to this day.
- It can still be useful for specific scenarios, such as when the logic and state that you want to share depend on a DOM element.

A very common example of the last use case would be tracking scroll in an area:

```
const ScrollDetector = ({ children }) => {
  const [scroll, setScroll] = useState();

  return (
    <div
      onScroll={(e) => setScroll(e.currentTarget.scrollTop)}
    >
      {children}
    </div>
  );
};
```

Exactly the same situation as before: you have some value, and you want to share that value with other components. Props again will be messy. And extracting it to a hook won't be as straightforward as before: you need to attach the `onScroll` listener to a `div` this time, not `window`. So you'd need to either introduce a Ref and pass it around (more about Refs in *Chapter 9. Refs: from storing data to imperative API*). Or just use the render prop pattern:

```
const ScrollDetector = ({ children }) => {
  const [scroll, setScroll] = useState();

  return (
    <div
      onScroll={(e) => setScroll(e.currentTarget.scrollTop)}
    >
```

```
      {children(scroll)}
    </div>
  );
};
```

And use it where you need to do something based on how much the user scrolled:

```
const Layout = () => {
  return (
    <ScrollDetector>
      {(scroll) => {
        return <>{scroll > 30 ? <SomeBlock /> : null}</>;
      }}
    </ScrollDetector>
  );
};
```

Interactive example and full code
https://advanced-react.com/examples/04/06

Key takeaways

Hope all of this makes sense and the pattern is as clear as day now. A few things to remember from this chapter:

- If a component that has elements as props wants to have control over the props of those elements or pass state to them, you'll need to convert those elements into render props:

```
const Button = ({ renderIcon }) => {
  const [someState, setSomeState] = useState()
  const someProps = { ... };
  return <button>Submit {renderIcon(someProps, someState)}</button>;
};
```

```
<Button renderIcon={(props, state) => <IconComponent {...props}
someProps={state} /> } />
```

- Children also can be render props, including "nesting" syntax.

```
const Parent = ({ children }) => {
  return children(somedata);
};
```

- Render props were very useful when we needed to share stateful logic between components without lifting it up.
- But hooks replaced that use case in 99% of cases.
- Render props for sharing stateful logic and data can still be useful even today, for example, when this logic is attached to a DOM element.

Chapter 5. Memoization with useMemo, useCallback and React.memo

Now that we know the most important composition patterns and how they work, it's time to talk about performance some more. More precisely, let's discuss the topic that is strongly associated with improving performance in React, but in reality, doesn't work as we intend to at least half the time we're doing it. Memoization. Our favorite `useMemo` and `useCallback` hooks and the `React.memo` higher-order component.

And I'm not joking or exaggerating about half the time by the way. Doing memoization properly is *hard*, much harder than it seems. By the end of this chapter, hopefully, you'll agree with me. Here you'll learn:

- What is the problem we're trying to solve with memoization (and it's not performance per se!).
- How `useMemo` and `useCallback` work under the hood, and what is the difference between them.
- Why memoizing props on a component by itself is an anti-pattern.
- What `React.memo` is, why we need it, and what are the basic rules for using it successfully.
- How to use it properly with the "elements as children" pattern.
- What is the role of `useMemo` in expensive calculations.

The problem: comparing values

It's all about comparing values in JavaScript. Primitive values like strings or booleans we compare by their actual value:

```
const a = 1;
```

```
const b = 1;

a === b; // will be true, values are exactly the same
```

With objects and anything inherited from objects (like arrays or functions), it's a different story.

When we create a variable with an object `const a = { id: 1 }`, the value stored there is not the *actual* value. It's just a reference to some part of the memory that holds that object. When we create another variable with the same data `const b = { id: 1 }`, it will be stored in another part of memory. And since it's a different part, the reference to it will also be different.

So even if these objects look exactly the same, the values in our fresh `a` and `b` variables are *different*: they point to different objects in memory. As a result, a simple comparison between them will always return false:

```
const a = { id: 1 };
const b = { id: 1 };

a === b; // will always be false
```

To make the comparison of `a === b` return `true`, we need to make sure that the reference in `b` is exactly the same as the reference in `a`. Something like this:

```
const a = { id: 1 };
const b = a;

a === b; // now will be true
```

This is what React has to deal with any time it needs to compare values between re-renders. It does this comparison every time we use hooks with dependencies, like in `useEffect` for example:

```
const Component = () => {
  const submit = () => {};
```

```
useEffect(() => {
  // call the function here
  submit();

  // it's declared outside of the useEffect
  // so should be in the dependencies
}, [submit]);

return ...
}
```

In this example, the `submit` function is declared outside of the
`useEffect` hook. So if I want to use it inside the hook, it should be
declared as a dependency. But since `submit` is declared locally inside
`Component`, it will be re-created every time `Component` re-renders.
Remember we discussed in *Chapter 2. Elements, children as props, and re-
renders* - a re-render is just React calling the component's functions. Every
local variable during that will be re-created, exactly the same as any
function in JavaScript.

So React will compare `submit` *before* and *after* re-render in order to
determine whether it should run the `useEffect` hook this time. The
comparison will always return `false` since it's a new reference each time.
As a result, the `useEffect` hook will be triggered on every re-render.

useMemo and useCallback: how they work

In order to battle that, we need a way to preserve the reference to the
`submit` function between re-renders. So that the comparison returns
`true` and the hook is not triggered unnecessarily. This is where
`useMemo` and `useCallback` hooks come in. Both have a similar API
and serve a similar purpose: to make sure that the reference in the variable
those hooks are assigned to changes only when the dependency of the hook
changes.

If I wrap that `submit` in `useCallback` :

```
const submit = useCallback(() => {
  // no dependencies, reference won't change between re-renders
}, []);
```

then the value in the `submit` variable will be the same reference between re-renders, the comparison will return `true` , and the `useEffect` hook that depends on it won't be triggered every time:

```
const Component = () => {
  const submit = useCallback(() => {
    // submit something here
  }, [])

  useEffect(() => {
    submit();

    // submit is memoized, so useEffect won't be triggered on every
  re-render
  }, [submit]);

  return ...
}
```

Exactly the same story with `useMemo` , only in this case, I need to *return* the function I want to memoize:

```
const submit = useMemo(() => {
  return () => {
    // this is out submit function - it's returned from the function
  that is passed to memo
  };
}, []);
```

Interactive example and full code
https://advanced-react.com/examples/05/01

As you can see, there is a slight difference in the API. `useCallback` accepts the function that we want to memoize as the first argument, while `useMemo` accepts a function and memoizes its return value. There is also a slight difference in their behavior because of that.

Since both hooks accept a function as the first argument, and since we declare these functions inside a React component, that means on every re-render, this function as the first argument will always be re-created. It's your normal JavaScript, nothing to do with React. If I declare a function that accepts another function as an argument and then call it multiple times with an inline function, that inline function will be re-created from scratch with each call.

```
// function that accepts a function as a first argument
const func = (callback) => {
  // do something with this callback here
};

// function as an argument - first call
func(() => {});
// function as an argument - second call, new function as an argument
func(() => {});
```

And our hooks are just functions integrated into the React lifecycle, nothing more.

So in order to return exactly the same reference in the `useCallback` hook, React does something like this:

```
let cachedCallback;

const func = (callback) => {
  if (dependenciesEqual()) {
    return cachedCallback;
  }

  cachedCallback = callback;

  return callback;
```

```
};
```

It caches the very first function that is passed as an argument and then just returns it every time if the dependencies of the hook haven't changed. And if dependencies have changed, it updates the cache and returns the refreshed function.

With `useMemo` , it's pretty much the same, only instead of returning the function, React calls it and returns the result:

```
let cachedResult;

const func = (callback) => {
  if (dependenciesEqual()) {
    return cachedResult;
  }

  cachedResult = callback();

  return cachedResult;
};
```

The real implementation[3] is slightly more complex, of course, but this is the basic idea.

Why is all of this important? For real-world applications, it's not, other than for understanding the difference in the API. However, there is this belief that sometimes pops up here and there that `useMemo` is better for performance than `useCallback` , since `useCallback` re-creates the function passed to it with each re-render, and `useMemo` doesn't do that. As you can see, this is not true. The function in the first argument will be re-created for both of them.

The only time that I can think of where it *would* actually matter, in theory, is when we pass as the first argument not the function itself, but a result of another function execution hardcoded inline. Basically this:

```
const submit = useCallback(something(), []);
```

In this case, the `something` function will be called every re-render, even though the `submit` reference won't change. So avoid doing expensive calculations in those functions.

Antipattern: memoizing props

The second most popular use case for memoization hooks, after memoized values as dependencies, is passing them to props. You surely have seen code like this:

```
const Component = () => {
  const onClick = useCallback(() => {
    // do something on click
  }, []);

  return <button onClick={onClick}>click me</button>;
};
```

Unfortunately, this `useCallback` here is just useless. There is this widespread belief that even ChatGPT seems to hold, that memoizing props prevents components from re-rendering. But as we know already from the previous chapters, if a component re-renders, every component inside that component will also re-render.

So whether we wrap our `onClick` function in `useCallback` or not *doesn't matter at all* here. All we did was make React do a little more work and make our code a little harder to read. When it's just one `useCallback`, it doesn't look that bad. But it's never just one, is it? There will be another, then another, they will start depending on each other, and before you know it, the logic in the app is just buried under the incomprehensible and undebuggable mess of `useMemo` and `useCallback`.

There are only two major use cases where we actually need to memoize props on a component. The first one is when this prop is used as a dependency in another hook in the downstream component.

```
const Parent = () => {
  // this needs to be memoized!
  // Child uses it inside useEffect
  const fetch = () => {};

  return <Child onMount={fetch} />;
};

const Child = ({ onMount }) => {
  useEffect(() => {
    onMount();
  }, [onMount]);
};
```

This should be self-explanatory: if a non-primitive value goes into a dependency, it should have a stable reference between re-renders, even if it comes from a chain of props.

And the second one is when a component is wrapped in `React.memo`.

What is React.memo

`React.memo` or just `memo` is a very useful util that React gives us. It allows us to memoize the *component itself*. If a component's re-render is triggered by its parent (and only then), and if this component is wrapped in `React.memo`, then and only then will React stop and check its props. If none of the props change, then the component will not be re-rendered, and the normal chain of re-renders will be stopped.

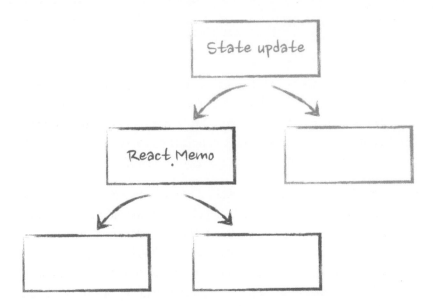

This is again the case when React performs that comparison we talked about at the beginning of the chapter. If even one of the props has changed, then the component wrapped in `React.memo` will be re-rendered as usual:

```
const Child = ({ data, onChange }) => {};
const ChildMemo = React.memo(Child);

const Component = () => {
  // object and function declared inline
  // will change with every re-render
  return <ChildMemo data={{ ...some_object }} onChange={() => {...}}
/>
}
```

And in the case of the example above, `data` and `onChange` are declared inline, so they will change with every re-render.

This is where `useMemo` and `useCallback` shine:

```
const Child = ({ data, onChange }) => {};
```

```
const ChildMemo = React.memo(Child);

const Component = () => {
  const data = useMemo(() => ({ ... }), []); // some object
  const onChange = useCallback(() => {}, []); // some callback

  // data and onChange now have stable reference
  // re-renders of ChildMemo will be prevented
  return <ChildMemo data={data} onChange={onChange} />
}
```

By memoizing `data` and `onChange`, we're preserving the reference to those objects between re-renders. Now, when React compares props on the `ChildMemo` component, the check will pass, and the component won't re-render.

Interactive example and full code
https://advanced-react.com/examples/05/02

But making sure that *all* props are memoized is not as easy as it sounds. We're doing it wrong in so many cases! And just one single mistake leads to broken props check, and as a result - every `React.memo`, `useCallback`, and `useMemo` become completely useless.

React.memo and props from props

The first and simplest case of broken memoization is props that are passed from props. Especially when the spreading of props in components in between is involved. Imagine you have a chain of components like this:

```
const Child = () => {};
const ChildMemo = React.memo(Child);

const Component = (props) => {
  return <ChildMemo {...props} />;
};
```

```
const ComponentInBetween = (props) => {
  return <Component {...props} />;
};


const InitialComponent = (props) => {
  // this one will have state and will trigger re-render of Component
  return (
    <ComponentInBetween {...props} data={{ id: '1' }} />
  );
};
```

How likely do you think that those who need to add that additional data to
the `InitialComponent` will go through every single component inside,
and deeper and deeper, to check whether any of them is wrapped in
`React.memo` ? Especially if all of those are spread among different files
and are quite complicated in implementation. Never going to happen.

But as a result, the `InitialComponent` breaks the memoization of the
`ChildMemo` component since it passes a non-memoized `data` prop to it.

Interactive example and full code
https://advanced-react.com/examples/05/03

So unless you're prepared and able to enforce the rule that *every single
prop everywhere* should be memoized, using the `React.memo` function
on components has to follow certain rules.

Rule 1: never spread props that are coming from other components.

Instead of this:

```
const Component = (props) => {
  return <ChildMemo {...props} />;
};
```

it has to be something explicit like this:

```
const Component = (props) => {
  return <ChildMemo some={prop.some} other={props.other} />;
};
```

Rule 2: avoid passing non-primitive props that are coming from other components.

Even the explicit example like the one above is still quite fragile. If any of those props are non-memoized objects or functions, memoization will break again.

Rule 3: avoid passing non-primitive values that are coming from custom hooks.

This seems almost contradictory to the generally accepted practice of extracting stateful logic into custom hooks. But their convenience is a double-edged sword here: they surely hide complexities away, but also hide away whether the data or functions have stable references as well. Consider this:

```
const Component = () => {
  const { submit } = useForm();

  return <ChildMemo onChange={submit} />;
};
```

The `submit` function is hidden in the `useForm` custom hook. And every custom hook will be triggered on every re-render. Can you tell from the code above whether it's safe to pass that `submit` to our `ChildMemo` ?

Nope, you can't. And chances are, it will look something like this:

```
const useForm = () => {
  // lots and lots of code to control the form state

  const submit = () => {
    // do something on submit, like data validation
  };
```

```
  return {
    submit,
  };
};
```

By passing that `submit` function to our `ChildMemo` , we just broke its memoization - from now on, it will re-render as if it's not wrapped in `React.memo` .

> **Interactive example and full code**
> https://advanced-react.com/examples/05/04

See how fragile this pattern is already? It gets worse.

React.memo and children

Let's take a look at this code:

```
const ChildMemo = React.memo(Child);

const Component = () => {
  return (
    <ChildMemo>
      <div>Some text here</div>
    </ChildMemo>
  );
};
```

Seems innocent enough: a memoized component with no props, renders some div inside, right? Well, memoization is broken here again, and the `React.memo` wrapper is completely useless.

Remember what we discussed in *Chapter 2. Elements, children as props, and re-renders*? This nice nesting syntax is nothing more than syntax sugar for the `children` prop. I can just rewrite this code like this:

```
const Component = () => {
  return <ChildMemo children={<div>Some text here</div>} />;
};
```

and it will behave exactly the same. And as we covered in *Chapter 2. Elements, children as props, and re-renders*, everything that is JSX is just syntax sugar for `React.createElement` and actually just an object. In this case, it will be an object with the type "div":

```
{
  type: "div",
  ... // the rest of the stuff
}
```

So what we have here from a memoization and props perspective is a component that is wrapped in `React.memo` and has a prop with a non-memoized object in it!

In order to fix it, we need to memoize the `div` as well:

```
const Component = () => {
  const content = useMemo(
    () => <div>Some text here</div>,
    [],
  );

  return <ChildMemo children={content} />;
};
```

or, back to the pretty syntax:

```
const Component = () => {
  const content = useMemo(
    () => <div>Some text here</div>,
    [],
  );

  return <ChildMemo>{content}</ChildMemo>;
```

```
};
```

Interactive example and full code
https://advanced-react.com/examples/05/05

Exactly the same story applies to children as a render prop, by the way. This
will be broken:

```
const Component = () => {
  return (
    <ChildMemo>{() => <div>Some text here</div>}</ChildMemo>
  );
};
```

Our children here is a *function* that is re-created on every re-render. Also
need to memoize it with `useMemo`:

```
const Component = () => {
  const content = useMemo(
    () => () => <div>Some text here</div>,
    [],
  );

  return <ChildMemo>{content}</ChildMemo>;
};
```

Or just use `useCallback`:

```
const Component = () => {
  const content = useCallback(
    () => <div>Some text here</div>,
    [],
  );

  return <ChildMemo>{content}</ChildMemo>;
};
```

Interactive example and full code
https://advanced-react.com/examples/05/06

Take a look at your app right now. How many of these have slipped through the cracks?

React.memo and memoized children (almost)

If you went through your app, fixed all those patterns, and feel confident that memoization is in a good state now, don't rush. When has life ever been so easy! What do you think about this one? Is it okay or broken?

```
const ChildMemo = React.memo(Child);
const ParentMemo = React.memo(Parent);

const Component = () => {
  return (
    <ParentMemo>
      <ChildMemo />
    </ParentMemo>
  );
};
```

Both of them are memoized, so it has to be okay, right? *Wrong.*
`ParentMemo` will behave as if it is not wrapped in `React.memo` - its children are actually not memoized!

Let's take a closer look at what's happening. As we already know, Elements are just syntax sugar for `React.createElement` , which returns an object with the type that points to the component. If I were creating a `<Parent />` Element, it would be this:

```
{
  type: Parent,
  ... // the rest of React stuff
```

}

With memoized components, *it's exactly the same*. The `<ParentMemo />` element will be converted into an object of a similar shape. Only the "type" property will contain information about our `ParentMemo`.

And this object is just an object, it's not memoized by itself. So again, from the memoization and props perspective, we have a `ParentMemo` component that has a `children` prop that contains a *non-memoized object*. Hence, broken memoization on `ParentMemo`.

To fix it, we need to memoize the object itself:

```
const Component = () => {
  const child = useMemo(() => <ChildMemo />, []);

  return <ParentMemo>{child}</ParentMemo>;
};
```

And then we might not even need the `ChildMemo` at all. Depends on its content and our intentions, of course. At least for the purpose of preventing `ParentMemo` from re-rendering, `ChildMemo` is unnecessary, and it can return back to being just a normal `Child`:

```
const Component = () => {
  const child = useMemo(() => <Child />, []);

  return <ParentMemo>{child}</ParentMemo>;
};
```

Interactive example and full code
https://advanced-react.com/examples/05/07

useMemo and expensive calculations

And the final, quite popular performance-related use case for `useMemo` is memoizing "expensive calculations." In quotes, since it's actually misused quite often as well.

First of all, what is an "expensive calculation"? Is concatenating strings expensive? Or sorting an array of 300 items? Or running a regular expression on a text of 5000 words? I don't know. And you don't. And no one knows until it's actually measured:

- on a device that is representative of your user base
- in context
- in comparison with the rest of the stuff that is happening at the same time
- in comparison with how it was before or the ideal state

Sorting an array of 300 items on my laptop, even with a 6x slowed-down CPU, takes less than 2ms. But on some old Android 2 mobile phone, it might take a second.

Executing a regular expression on a text that takes 100ms feels slow. But if it's run as a result of a button click, once in a blue moon, buried somewhere deep in the settings screen, then it's almost instant. A regular expression that takes 30ms to run seems fast enough. But if it's run on the main page on every mouse move or scroll event, it's unforgivably slow and needs to be improved.

It always *depends*. "Measure first" should be the default thinking when there is an urge to wrap something in `useMemo` because it's an "expensive calculation."

The second thing to think about is React. In particular, rendering of components in comparison to raw JavaScript calculations. More likely than not, anything that is calculated within `useMemo` will be an order of magnitude faster than re-rendering actual elements anyway. For example, sorting that array of 300 items on my laptop took less than 2ms. Re-rendering list elements from that array, even when they were just simple buttons with some text, took more than 20ms. If I want to improve the performance of that component, the best thing to do would be to get rid of the unnecessary re-renders of everything, not memoizing something that takes less than 2ms.

So an addition to the "measure first" rule, when it comes to memoization, should be: "don't forget to measure how long it takes to re-render component elements as well." And if you wrap every JavaScript calculation in `useMemo` and gain 10ms from it, but re-rendering of actual components still takes almost 200ms, then what's the point? All it does is complicate the code without any visible gain.

And finally, `useMemo` is only useful for *re-renders*. That's the whole point of it and how it works. If your component never re-renders, then `useMemo` just does nothing.

More than nothing, it forces React to do additional work on the initial render. Don't forget: the very first time the `useMemo` hook runs, when the component is first mounted, React needs to cache it. It will use a little bit of memory and computational power for that, which otherwise would be free. With just one `useMemo`, the impact won't be measurable, of course. But in large apps, with hundreds of them scattered everywhere, it actually can measurably slow down the initial render. It will be death by a thousand cuts in the end.

Key takeaways

Well, that's depressing. Does all of this mean we shouldn't use memoization? Not at all. It can be a very valuable tool in our performance battle. But considering so many caveats and complexities that surround it, I would recommend using composition-based optimization techniques as much as possible first. `React.memo` should be the last resort when all other things have failed.

And let's remember:

- React compares objects/arrays/functions by their reference, not their value. That comparison happens in hooks' dependencies and in props of components wrapped in `React.memo`.

- The inline function passed as an argument to either `useMemo` or `useCallback` will be re-created on every re-render. `useCallback` memoizes that function itself, `useMemo` memoizes the result of its execution.
- Memoizing props on a component makes sense only when:
    - This component is wrapped in `React.memo`.
    - This component uses those props as dependencies in any of the hooks.
    - This component passes those props down to other components, and they have either of the situations from above.
- If a component is wrapped in `React.memo` and its re-render is triggered by its parent, then React will not re-render this component if its props haven't changed. In any other case, re-render will proceed as usual.
- Memoizing all props on a component wrapped in `React.memo` is harder than it seems. Avoid passing non-primitive values that are coming from other props or hooks to it.
- When memoizing props, remember that "children" is also a non-primitive prop that needs to be memoized.

Chapter 6. Deep dive into diffing and reconciliation

In the previous chapters, we covered the basics of React's reconciliation and diffing algorithms. We now know that when we create React Elements, such as `const a = <Child />`, we're actually creating objects. The HTML-like syntax (JSX) is just syntax sugar that is transformed into the `React.createElement` function. That function returns a description object with the `type` property that points to either a component, a memoized component, or a string with an HTML tag.

Also, we know that if the reference to that object itself changes between re-renders, then React will re-render this Element if its `type` remains the same and the component in `type` is not memoized with `React.memo`.

But this is just the beginning. There are more variables and moving pieces here, and understanding this process in detail is very important. It will allow us to fix some very not-obvious bugs, implement the most performant lists, reset the state when we need it, and avoid one of the biggest performance killers in React. All in one go. None of it seems connected at first glance, but all of this is part of the same story: how React determines which components need to be re-rendered, which components need to be removed, and which ones need to be added to the screen.

In this chapter, we'll investigate a few very curious bugs, dive very deep into how things work under the hood, and in the process of doing so, we will learn:

- How React's Diffing and Reconciliation algorithm works.
- What happens when a state update is triggered and React needs to re-render components.
- Why we shouldn't create components inside other components.
- How to solve the bug of two different components sharing the same state.

- How React renders arrays and how we can influence that.
- What is the purpose of the "key" attribute.
- How to write the most performant lists possible.
- Why we would use the "key" attribute outside of dynamic lists.

The Mysterious Bug

Let's start with a little mystery to keep things interesting.

Imagine you render a component conditionally. If "something" is `true`, show me this component. Otherwise, show me something else. For example, I'm developing a "sign up" form for my website, and part of that form is whether those who sign up are a company or just a regular human fellow, for some crazy tax purposes. So I want to show the "Company Tax ID" input field only after the user clicks the "yes, I'm signing up as a company" checkbox. And for people, show a text "You don't have to give us your tax ID, lucky human."

The code for this app will look something like this:

```
const Form = () => {
  const [isCompany, setIsCompany] = useState(false);

  return (
    <>
      {/* checkbox somewhere here */}
      {isCompany ? (
        <Input id="company-tax-id-number" placeholder="Enter you
company ID" ... />
      ) : (
        <TextPlaceholder />
      )}
    </>
  )
}
```

What will happen here from a re-rendering and mounting perspective if the user actually claims that they are a company and the value `isCompany` changes from the default `false` to `true` ?

No surprises here, and the answer is pretty intuitive: the `Form` component
will re-render itself, the `TextPlaceholder` component will be
unmounted, and the `Input` component will be mounted. If I flip the
checkbox back, the `Input` will be unmounted again, and the
`TextPlaceholder` will be mounted.

From a behavioral perspective, all of this means that if I type something in
the `Input` , flip the checkbox, and then flip it back, whatever I typed there
will be lost. `Input` has its own internal state to hold the text, which will be
destroyed when it unmounts and will be re-created from scratch when it
mounts back.

But what will happen if I actually *need* to collect the tax ID from people as
well? And the field should look and behave exactly the same, but it will have
a different `id` , different `onChange` callback, and other different settings.
Naturally, I'd do something like this:

```
const Form = () => {
  const [isCompany, setIsCompany] = useState(false);

  return (
    <>
      {/* checkbox somewhere here */}
      {isCompany ? (
        <Input id="company-tax-id-number" placeholder="Enter you
company Tax ID" ... />
      ) : (
        <Input id="person-tax-id-number" placeholder="Enter you
personal Tax ID" ... />
      )}
    </>
  )
}
```

What will happen here now?

The answer is, of course, again pretty intuitive and exactly as any sensible
person would expect... The unmounting doesn't happen anymore! If I type

something in the field and then flip the checkbox, the text is still there! React thinks that both of those inputs are actually the same thing, and instead of unmounting the first one and mounting the second one, it just re-renders the first one with the new data from the second one.

> **Interactive example and full code**
> https://advanced-react.com/examples/06/01

If you're not surprised by this at all and can without hesitation say, "Ah, yeah, it's because of [the reason]," then wow, can I get your autograph? For the rest of us who got an eye twitch and a mild headache because of this behavior, it's time to dive into React's reconciliation process to get the answer.

Diffing and Reconciliation

It's all because of the DOM[4]. Or to be precise, the fact that we don't have to deal with it directly when we're writing React code. This is very convenient for us: instead of doing `appendChild` or comparing attributes manually, we just write components. And then React transforms whatever we give to it into DOM elements on the screen with appropriate data. When we write code like this:

```
const Input = ({ placeholder }) => {
  return (
    <input
      type="text"
      id="input-id"
      placeholder={placeholder}
    />
  );
};

// somewhere else
<Input placeholder="Input something here" />;
```

we expect React to add the normal HTML `input` tag with `placeholder` set in the appropriate place in the DOM structure. If we change the `placeholder` value in the React component, we expect React to update our DOM element with the new value and to see that value on the screen. Ideally, instantly. So, React can't just remove the previous input and append a new one with the new data. That would be terribly slow. Instead, it needs to identify that already existing input DOM element and just update its attributes. If we didn't have React, we'd have to do something like this:

```
const input = document.getElementById('input-id');
input.placeholder = 'new data';
```

In React, we don't have to; it handles it for us. It does so by creating and modifying what we sometimes call the "Virtual DOM." This Virtual DOM is just a giant object with all the components that are supposed to render, all their props, and their children - which are also objects of the same shape. Just a tree. What the `Input` component from the example above should render will be represented as something like this:

```
{
  type: "input", // type of element that we need to render
  props: {...}, // input's props like id or placeholder
  ... // bunch of other internal stuff
}
```

If our `Input` component was rendering something more:

```
const Input = () => {
  return (
    <>
      <label htmlFor="input-id">{label}</label>
      <input type="text" id="input-id" />
    </>
  );
};
```

then `label` and `input` from React's perspective would be just an array of those objects:

```
[
  {
    type: 'label',
    ... // other stuff
  },
  {
    type: 'input',
    ... // other stuff
  }
]
```

DOM elements like `input` or `label` will have their "type" as strings, and React will know to convert them to the DOM elements directly. But if we're rendering React components, they are not directly correlated with DOM elements, so React needs to work around that somehow.

```
const Component = () => {
  return <Input />;
};
```

In this case, it will put the component's function as the "type." It just grabs the entire function that we know as the `Input` component and puts it there:

```
{
  type: Input, // reference to that Input function we declared earlier
  ... // other stuff
}
```

And then, when React gets a command to mount the app (initial render), it iterates over that tree and does the following:

- If the "type" is a string, it generates the HTML element of that type.
- If the "type" is a function (i.e., our component), it calls it and iterates over the tree that this function returned.

Until it eventually gets the entire tree of DOM nodes that are ready to be shown. A component like this, for example:

```
const Component = () => {
  return (
    <div>
      <Input placeholder="Text1" id="1" />
      <Input placeholder="Text2" id="2" />
    </div>
  );
};
```

will be represented as:

```
{
  type: 'div',
  props: {
    // children are props!
    children: [
      {
        type: Input,
        props: { id: "1", placeholder: "Text1" }
      },
      {
        type: Input,
        props: { id: "2", placeholder: "Text2" }
      }
    ]
  }
}
```

Which will on mounting resolve into HTML like this:

```
<div>
  <input placeholder="Text1" id="1" />
  <input placeholder="Text2" id="2" />
</div>
```

Finally, when everything is ready, React appends those DOM elements to the actual `document` with JavaScript's `appendChild` [5] command.

Reconciliation and state update

After that, the fun begins. Suppose one of the components from that tree has state, and its update was triggered (re-render is triggered). React needs to update all the elements on the screen with the new data that comes from that state update. Or maybe add or remove some new elements.

So it begins its journey through that tree again, starting from where the state update was initiated. If we have this code:

```
const Component = () => {
  // return just one element
  return <Input />;
};
```

React will understand that the `Component` returns this object when rendered:

```
{
  type: Input,
  ... // other internal stuff
}
```

It will compare the "type" field of that object from "before" and "after" the state update. If the type is the same, the `Input` component will be marked as "needs update," and its re-render will be triggered. If the type has changed, then React, during the re-render cycle, will remove (unmount) the "previous" component and add (mount) the "next" component. In our case, the "type" will be the same since it's just a reference to a function, and that reference hasn't changed.

If I were doing something conditional with that `Input`, like returning another component:

```
const Component = () => {
  if (isCompany) return <Input />;

  return <TextPlaceholder />;
};
```

then, assuming that the update was triggered by `isCompany` value flipping from `true` to `false`, the objects that React will be comparing are:

```
// Before update, isCompany was "true"
{
  type: Input,
  ...
}

// After update, isCompany is "false"
{
  type: TextPlaceholder,
  ...
}
```

You guessed the result, right? "Type" has changed from `Input` to `TextPlaceholder` references, so React will unmount `Input` and remove everything associated with it from the DOM. And it will mount the new `TextPlaceholder` component and append it to the DOM for the first time. Everything that was associated with the `Input` field, including its state and everything you typed there, is destroyed.

Why we can't define components inside other components

Now that this behavior is clear, we can answer one very important question: why shouldn't we create components inside other components? Why is code like this usually considered an anti-pattern?

```
const Component = () => {
  const Input = () => <input />;

  return <Input />;
};
```

If we look at this code from the reconciliation and definition object perspective, this is what our `Component` returns:

```
{
  type: Input,
}
```

It's just an object that has a "type" property that points to a function. However, the function is created *inside* `Component`. It's local to it and will be recreated with every re-render as a result. So when React tries to compare those types, it will compare two different functions: one before re-render and one after re-render. And as we know from *Chapter 5. Memoization with useMemo, useCallback and React.memo*, we can't compare functions in JavaScript, not like this.

```
const a = () => {};
const b = () => {};

a === b; // will always be false
```

As a result, the "type" of that child will be different with every re-render, so React will remove the "previous" component and mount the "next" one.

If the component is heavy enough, we will even see a "flickering" effect on the screen: it will briefly disappear and then re-appear back. This is what we usually call re-mounting. And normally it's not intentional and it's terrible for performance - re-mounting will take at least twice as long as a normal re-render. In addition, since the "before" component and everything that is associated with it is destroyed, we'll see quite curious and hard-to-trace bugs as a result. If that component is supposed to hold state or focus, for example, those will disappear on every re-render.

In the associated code example above, you can see how it behaves: the input component triggers a re-render with every keystroke, and the "ComponentWithState" is re-mounted. As a result, if you click on that component to change its state to "active" and then start typing, that state will disappear.

Declaring components inside other components like this can be one of the biggest performance killers in React.

The answer to the mystery

Now let's return to the mysterious code from the beginning and solve that bug:

```
const Form = () => {
  const [isCompany, setIsCompany] = useState(false);

  return (
    <>
      {/*checkbox somewhere here*/}
      {isCompany ? (
        <Input id="company-tax-id-number" placeholder="Enter you
company Tax ID" ... />
      ) : (
        <Input id="person-tax-id-number" placeholder="Enter you
personal Tax ID" ... />
      )}
    </>
  )
}
```

If the `isCompany` variable changes from `true` to `false` here, which objects will be compared?

Before, `isCompany` is `true` :

```
{
    type: Input,
    ... // the rest of the stuff, including props like id="company-tax-
    id-number"
}
```

After, `isCompany` is `false` :

```
{
    type: Input,
    ... // the rest of the stuff, including props like id="person-tax-
    id-number"
}
```

From the React perspective, the "type" *hasn't changed.* Both of them have a reference to exactly the same function: the `Input` component. The only thing that has changed, thinks React, are the props: `id` changed from `"company-tax-id-number"` to `"person-tax-id-number"` , placeholder changed, and so on.

So, in this case, React does what it was taught: it simply takes the existing `Input` component and updates it with the new data. I.e., re-renders it. Everything that is associated with the existing `Input` , like its DOM element or state, is still there. Nothing is destroyed. This results in the behavior that we've seen: I type something in the input, flip the checkbox, and the text is still there.

This behavior isn't necessarily bad. I can see a situation where re-rendering instead of re-mounting is exactly what I would want. But in this case, I'd probably want to fix it and ensure that inputs are reset and re-mounted every time I switch between them: they are different entities from the business logic perspective, so I don't want to re-use them.

There are at least two easy ways to fix it: arrays and keys.

Reconciliation and arrays

Until now, I've only mentioned the fact of arrays in that data tree. But it's highly unlikely that anyone can write a React app where every single component returns only one element. We need to talk about arrays of elements and how they behave during re-renders in more detail now. Even our simple `Form` actually has an array:

```
const Form = () => {
  const [isCompany, setIsCompany] = useState(false);

  return (
    <>
      {/*checkbox somewhere here*/}
      {isCompany ? (
        <Input id="company-tax-id-number" ... />
      ) : (
        <Input id="person-tax-id-number" ... />
      )}
    </>
  )
}
```

It returns a Fragment (that thing: `<>...</>`) that has an *array* of children: there is a checkbox hidden there. The actual code is more like this:

```
const Form = () => {
  const [isCompany, setIsCompany] = useState(false);

  return (
    <>
      <Checkbox onChange={() => setIsCompany(!isCompany)} />
      {isCompany ? (
        <Input id="company-tax-id-number" ... />
      ) : (
        <Input id="person-tax-id-number" ... />
      )}
    </>
  )
```

```
  )
}
```

During re-render, when React sees an array of children instead of an individual item, it just iterates over it and then compares "before" and "after" elements and their "type" according to their position in the array.

Basically, if I flip the checkbox and trigger the `Form` re-render, React will see this array of items:

```
[
  {
    type: Checkbox,
  },
  {
    type: Input, // our conditional input
  },
];
```

and will go through them one by one. First element. "Type" before: `Checkbox`, "type" after: also `Checkbox`. Re-use it and re-render it. Second element. Same procedure. And so on.

Even if some of those elements are rendered conditionally like this:

```
isCompany ? <Input /> : null;
```

React will still have a stable number of items in that array. Just sometimes, those items will be `null`. If I re-write the `Form` like this:

```
const Form = () => {
  const [isCompany, setIsCompany] = useState(false);

  return (
    <>
      <Checkbox onChange={() => setIsCompany(!isCompany)} />
      {isCompany ? <Input id="company-tax-id-number" ... /> : null}
      {!isCompany ? <Input id="person-tax-id-number" ... /> : null}
    </>
```

```
    )
  }
```

it will be an array of always three items: `Checkbox`, `Input` or `null`, and `Input` or `null`.

So, what will happen here when the state changes and re-render runs throughout the form?

Before, `isCompany` is `false`:

```
[{ type: Checkbox }, null, { type: Input }];
```

After, `isCompany` is `true`:

```
[{ type: Checkbox }, { type: Input }, null];
```

And when React starts comparing them, item by item, it will be:

- the first item, `Checkbox` before and after → re-render `Checkbox`
- the second item, `null` before and `Input` after → mount `Input`
- third item, `Input` before, `null` after → unmount `Input`

And voila! Magically, by changing the inputs' position in the render output, without changing anything else in the logic, the bug is fixed, and inputs behave exactly as I would expect!

> **Interactive example and full code**
> https://advanced-react.com/examples/06/03

Reconciliation and "key"

There is another way to fix the same bug: with the help of the "key" attribute.

The "key" should be familiar to anyone who has written any lists in React. React forces us to add it when we iterate over arrays of data:

```javascript
const data = ['1', '2'];

const Component = () => {
  // "key" is mandatory here!
  return data.map((value) => <Input key={value} />);
};
```

The output of this component should be clear by now: just an array of objects with the "type" `Input` :

```javascript
[
  { type: Input }, // "1" data item
  { type: Input }, // "2" data item
];
```

But the problem with dynamic lists like this is that they are, well, *dynamic*. We can re-order them, add new items at the beginning or end, and generally mess around with them.

Now, React faces an interesting task: all components in that array are of the same type. How to detect which one is which? If the order of those items changes:

```javascript
[
  { type: Input }, // "2" data item now, but React doesn't know that
  { type: Input }, // "1" data item now, but React doesn't know that
];
```

how to make sure that the correct existing element is re-used? Because if it just relies on the order of elements in that array, it will re-use the instance of the first element for the data of the second element, and vice versa. This will result in weird behavior if those items have state: it will stay with the first item. If you type something in the first input field and re-order the array, the typed text will remain in the first input.

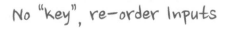

No "key", re-order Inputs

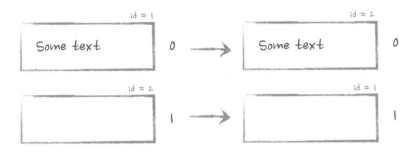

This is why we need "key": it's basically React's version of a unique identifier of an element within children's array that is used between re-renders. If an element has a "key" in parallel with "type," then during re-render, React will re-use the existing elements, with all their associated state and DOM, if the "key" and "type" match "before" and "after." Regardless of their position in the array.

With this array, the data would look like this. Before re-ordering:

```
[
  { type: Input, key: '1' }, // "1" data item
  { type: Input, key: '2' }, // "2" data item
];
```

After re-ordering:

```
[
  { type: Input, key: '2' }, // "2" data item, React knows that
because of "key"
  { type: Input, key: '1' }, // "1" data item, React knows that
because of "key"
];
```

Now, with the key present, React will know that after re-render, it needs to re-use an already created element that used to be in the first position. So it will just swap `input` DOM nodes around. And the text that we typed in the first element will move with it to the second position.

id as "key", re-order Inputs

Interactive example and full code
https://advanced-react.com/examples/06/04

"Key" attribute and memoized list

One of the most common misconceptions about the `key` attribute and lists is that `key` is needed there for performance reasons. That adding `key` to the dynamic array prevents array items from re-rendering. As you can see from the above, that's not how the `key` works. `Key` helps React to identify which already existing instance it should re-use when it re-renders those items. *Re-render* will still happen, like with any components rendered inside another component.

If we want to prevent re-renders of items, we need to use `React.memo` for that. For static arrays (those that don't change their elements or their position), it's very easy: just wrap whatever the item element is in `React.memo` and use either some sort of `id` property of that item or just the array's index in the `key`. Anything that is stable between re-renders will do.

```
const data = [
  { id: 'business', placeholder: 'Business Tax' },
  { id: 'person', placeholder: 'Person Tax' },
];
const InputMemo = React.memo(Input);
const Component = () => {
  // array's index is fine here, the array is static
  return data.map((value, index) => (
    <InputMemo
      key={index}
      placeholder={value.placeholder}
    />
  ));
};
```

If the re-render of the `Parent` is triggered, none of the `InputMemo` components will re-render: they are wrapped in `React.memo`, and the key for any of the items hasn't changed.

With dynamic arrays, it's a bit more interesting, and this is where the `key` plays a crucial role. What will happen here if what triggered the re-render is the *re-ordering* of that array?

```
// array before re-render
[
  { id: 'business', placeholder: 'Business Tax' },
  { id: 'person', placeholder: 'Person Tax' },
]

// array after re-render
[
  { id: 'person', placeholder: 'Person Tax' },
  { id: 'business', placeholder: 'Business Tax' },
]
```

If we just use the array's `index` as a `key` again, then from React's perspective, the item with the `key="0"` will be the first item in the array before and after the re-render. But the prop `placeholder` will change: it will transition from "Business Tax" to "Person Tax." As a result, even if this item is memoized, from React's perspective, the prop on it changed, so it will re-render it as if memoization doesn't exist!

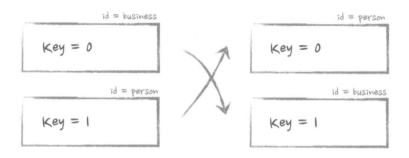

Inputs memoized, index as key, re-order

id = business

key = 0

id = person

key = 1

id = person

key = 0

id = business

key = 1

everyone re-renders

The fix for this is simple: we need to make sure that the `key` matches the item it identifies. In our case, we can just put the `id` there:

```
const Parent = () => {
  // if array can be sorted, or number of its items can change, then
  "index" as "key" is not a good idea
  // we need to use something that identifies an array item instead
  return sortedData.map((value, index) => (
    <InputMemo
      key={value.id}
      placeholder={value.placeholder}
    />
  ));
};
```

If the data has nothing unique like an `id`, then we'd need to iterate over that array somewhere outside of the component that re-renders and add that `id` there manually.

In the case of our inputs, if we use the `id` for `key`, the item with the `key="business"` will still have the prop `placeholder="Business`

Tax," just in a different place in the array. So React will just swap the associated DOM nodes around, but the actual component *won't re-render*.

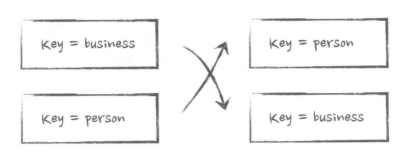

And exactly the same story happens if we were adding another input at the beginning of the array. If we use the array's `index` as `key`, then the item with the `key="0"`, from React's perspective, will just change its `placeholder` prop from "Business Tax" to "New tax"; `key="1"` item will transition from "Person Tax" to "Business Tax". So they both will re-render. And the new item with the `key="2"` and the text "Person Tax" will be mounted from scratch.

Inputs memoized, index as key, add new

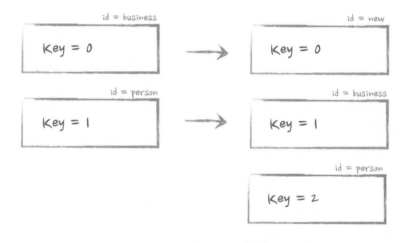

re-render, mounted

And if we use the `id` as a `key` instead, then both "Business Tax" and "Person Tax" will keep their keys, and since they are memoized, they won't re-render. And the new item, with the `key` "New tax", will be mounted from scratch.

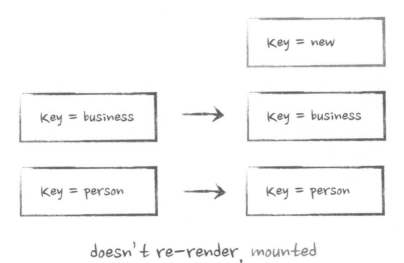

Inputs memoized, id as key, add new

Key = new

Key = business ⟶ Key = business

Key = person ⟶ Key = person

doesn't re-render, mounted

Interactive example and full code
https://advanced-react.com/examples/06/05

State reset technique

Why does all of this logic with `keys` matter for our `Form` component and its bug from the very beginning of the chapter? Fun fact: "key" is just an attribute of an element, it's not limited to dynamic arrays. In any children's array, it will behave exactly the same way. And as we already found out, the object definition of our `Form` with the bug from the very beginning:

```
const Form = () => {
  const [isCompany, setIsCompany] = useState(false);

  return (
    <>
```

```
      <Checkbox onChange={() => setIsCompany(!isCompany)} />
      {isCompany ? (
        <Input id="company-tax-id-number" ... />
      ) : (
        <Input id="person-tax-id-number" ... />
      )}
    </>
  )
}
```

has an array of children:

```
[
  { type: Checkbox },
  { type: Input }, // react thinks it's the same input between re-
renders
];
```

All we need to fix the initial bug is to make React realize that those `Input` components between re-renders are actually *different* components and should not be re-used. If we add a "key" to those inputs, we'll achieve exactly that.

```
{isCompany ? (
  <Input id="company-tax-id-number" key="company-tax-id-number" ... />
) : (
  <Input id="person-tax-id-number" key="person-tax-id-number" ... />
)}
```

Now, the array of children before and after re-render will change.

Before, `isCompany` is `false` :

```
[
  { type: Checkbox },
  {
    type: Input,
    key: 'person-tax-id-number',
  },
```

```
];
```

After, `isCompany` is `true`:

```
[
  { type: Checkbox },
  {
    type: Input,
    key: 'company-tax-id-number',
  },
];
```

Voila, the keys are different! React will drop the first `Input` and mount from scratch the second one. State is now reset to empty when we switch between inputs.

Interactive example and full code
https://advanced-react.com/examples/06/06

This technique is known as "state reset". It has nothing to do with state per se, but it's sometimes used when there is a need to reset the state of an uncontrolled component (like an input field) to a default value. You don't even have to have two components for this, like I had above. One will do. Any unique value in `key` that changes depending on your conditions will work for this. If you want to force state reset on URL change, for example, it could be as simple as this:

```
const Component = () => {
  // grab the current url from our router solution
  const { url } = useRouter();

  // I want to reset that input field when the page URL changes
  return <Input id="some-id" key={url} />;
};
```

But be careful here, though. It's not just "state reset" as you can see. It forces React to unmount a component completely and mount a new one from scratch. For big components, that might cause performance problems. The fact that the state is reset is just a by-product of this total destruction.

Using "key" to force reuse of an existing element

Another fun fact: if we actually *needed* to reuse an existing element, "key" could help with that as well. Remember this code, where we fixed the bug by rendering the `Input` element in different positions in the children array?

```
const Form = () => {
  const [isCompany, setIsCompany] = useState(false);

  return (
    <>
      <Checkbox onChange={() => setIsCompany(!isCompany)} />
      {isCompany ? <Input id="company-tax-id-number" ... /> : null}
      {!isCompany ? <Input id="person-tax-id-number" ... /> : null}
    </>
  )
}
```

When the `isCompany` state variable changes, `Input` components will unmount and mount since they are in different positions in the array. But! If I add the "key" attribute to both of those inputs with the same value, the magic happens.

```
<>
  <Checkbox onChange={() => setIsCompany(!isCompany)} />
  {isCompany ? <Input id="company-tax-id-number" key="tax-input" ...
/> : null}
  {!isCompany ? <Input id="person-tax-id-number" key="tax-input" ...
/> : null}
</>
```

From the data and re-renders' perspective, it will now be like this.

Before, `isCompany` is `false`:

```
[
  { type: Checkbox },
  null,
  {
    type: Input,
    key: 'tax-input',
  },
];
```

After, `isCompany` is `true`:

```
[
  { type: Checkbox },
  { type: Input, key: "tax-input" }
  null
]
```

React sees an array of children and sees that before and after re-renders, there is an element with the `Input` type and the same "key." So it will think that the `Input` component just changed its position in the array and will re-use the already created instance for it. If we type something, the state is preserved even though the `Input` s are technically different.

> **Interactive example and full code**
> https://advanced-react.com/examples/06/07

For this particular example, it's just a curious behavior, of course, and not very useful in practice. But I could imagine it being used for fine-tuning the performance of components like accordions, tabs content, or some galleries.

Why we don't need keys outside of arrays?

Let's have a bit more fun with reconciliation, now that the mystery is solved and the algorithm is more or less clear. There are still a few mini-questions and mysteries there. For example, have you noticed that React never forced you to add keys to anything unless you're iterating over an array?

The object definition of this:

```
const data = ['1', '2'];

const Component = () => {
  // "key" is mandatory here!
  return (
    <>
      {data.map((value) => (
        <Input key={value} />
      ))}
    </>
  );
};
```

and this:

```
const Component = () => {
  // no-one cares about "key" here
  return (
    <>
      <Input />
      <Input />
    </>
  );
};
```

will be exactly the same, just a fragment with two inputs as a children array:

```
[{ type: Input }, { type: Input }];
```

So why, in one case, do we need a "key" for React to behave, and in another - don't?

The difference is that the first example is a dynamic array. React doesn't know what you will do with this array during the next re-render: remove, add, or rearrange items, or maybe leave them as-is. So it forces you to add the "key" as a precautionary measure, in case you're messing with the array on the fly.

Where is the fun here, you might ask? Here it is: try to render those inputs that are not in an array with the same "key," applied conditionally:

```
const Component = () => {
  const [isReverse, setIsReverse] = useState(false);
  // no-one cares about "key" here
  return (
    <>
      <Input key={isReverse ? 'some-key' : null} />
      <Input key={!isReverse ? 'some-key' : null} />
    </>
  );
};
```

Try to predict what will happen if I type something in those inputs and toggle the boolean on and off.

Interactive example and full code
https://advanced-react.com/examples/06/08

Dynamic arrays and normal elements together

If you've read the entire chapter carefully, there's a possibility that by now you might have had a minor heart attack. I certainly had one when I was investigating all of this. Because...

- If dynamic items are transformed into an array of children that is no different than normal elements stuck together,
- and if I put normal items after a dynamic array,
- and add or remove an item in the array,

does it mean that items after this array will always re-mount themselves?? Basically, is this code a performance disaster or not?

```
const data = ['1', '2'];

const Component = () => {
  return (
    <>
      {data.map((i) => (
        <Input key={i} id={i} />
      ))}
      {/* will this input re-mount if I add a new item in the array
above? */}
      <Input id="3" />
    </>
  );
};
```

Because *if* this is transformed into an array of three children - the first two are dynamic, and the last one static - it will be. If this is the case, then the definition object will be this:

```
[
  { type: Input, key: 1 }, // input from the array
  { type: Input, key: 2 }, // input from the array
  { type: Input }, // input after the array
];
```

And if I add another item to the `data` array, on the third position there will be an `Input` element with the `key="3"` from the array, and the "manual" input will move to the fourth position, which would mean from the React perspective that it's a new item that needs to be mounted.

Luckily, this is not the case. Phew... React is smarter than that.

When we mix dynamic and static elements, like in the code above, React simply creates an array of those dynamic elements and makes that entire array the very first child in the children's array. This is going to be the definition object for that code:

```
[
  // the entire dynamic array is the first position in the children's
  array
  [
    { type: Input, key: 1 },
    { type: Input, key: 2 },
  ],
  {
    type: Input, // this is our manual Input after the array
  },
];
```

Our manual `Input` will always have the second position here. There will be no re-mounting. No performance disaster. The heart attack was uncalled for.

Key takeaways

Ooof, that was a long chapter! Hope you had fun with the investigation and the mysteries and learned something cool while doing so. A few things to remember from all of that:

- React will compare elements between re-renders with elements in the same place in the returned array on any level of hierarchy. The first one with the first one, the second with the second, etc.
- If the type of the element and its position in the array is the same, React will re-render that element. If the type changes at that position, then React will unmount the previous component and mount the new one.
- An array of children will always have the same number of children (if it's not dynamic). Conditional elements (`isSomething ? <A /> : <B />`) will take just one place, even if one of them is `null` .

- If the array is dynamic, then React can't reliably identify those elements between re-renders. So we use the `key` attribute to help it. This is important when the array can change the number of its items or their position between re-renders (re-order, add, remove), and especially important if those elements are wrapped in `React.memo`.
- We can use the `key` outside of dynamic arrays as well to force React to recognize elements at the same position in the array with the same type as different. Or to force it to recognize elements at different positions with the same type as the same.
- We can also force unmounting of a component with a `key` if that key changes between re-renders based on some information (like routing). This is sometimes called "state reset".

Chapter 7. Higher-order components in modern world

There is one final composition technique that we need to discuss before moving on to other parts of React: higher-order components! Before hooks took over, this was one of the most popular patterns for sharing stateful logic and context data. It's still used here and there even today, especially in older libraries or in projects that started their life before hooks. So while it's probably not the best idea to introduce them in new code, understanding what they are and how they work is still more or less mandatory.

So let's start from the beginning and learn in the process:

- What is a higher-order component pattern?
- How can we use higher-order components to enhance callbacks and React lifecycle events?
- Different ways to pass data to higher-order components.
- How to create reusable components that intercept DOM and keyboard events.

What is a higher-order component?

According to the React docs, a Higher-Order Component[6] is an advanced technique for reusing component logic that is used for cross-cutting concerns.

In English, it's a function that accepts a component as one of its arguments, executes some logic, and then returns another component that renders the component from the argument. The simplest variant of it, that does nothing, is this:

```
// accept a Component as an argument
```

```
const withSomeLogic = (Component) => {
  // do something

  // return a component that renders the component from the argument
  return (props) => <Component {...props} />;
};
```

The key here is the return part of the function - it's just a component, like
any other component.

And then, when it's time to use it, it would look like this:

```
// just a button
const Button = ({ onClick }) => (
  <button onClick={onClick}>Button</button>
);

// same button, but with enhanced functionality
const ButtonWithSomeLogic = withSomeLogic(Button);
```

You pass your `Button` component to the function, and it returns the new
`Button` , which includes whatever logic is defined in the higher-order
component. And then this button can be used like any other button:

```
const SomePage = () => {
  return (
    <>
      <Button />
      <ButtonWithSomeLogic />
    </>
  );
};
```

The simplest and most common use case would be to inject props into
components. We can, for example, implement a `withTheming`
component that extracts the current theme of the website (dark or light
mode) and sends that value into the `theme` prop. It would look like this:

```
const withTheme = (Component) => {
```

```
  // isDark will come from something like context
  const theme = isDark ? 'dark' : 'light';

  // making sure that we pass all props to the component back
  // and also inject the new one: theme
  return (props) => <Component {...props} theme={theme} />;
};
```

And now, if we use it on our button, it will have the `theme` prop available for use:

```
const Button = ({ theme }) => {
  // theme prop here will come from withTheme HOC below
  return <button className={theme} ...>Button</button>
}

const ButtonWithTheme = withTheme(Button);
```

Interactive example and full code
https://advanced-react.com/examples/07/01

Before the introduction of hooks, higher-order components were widely used for accessing context and any external data subscriptions. Redux's old `connect` [7] or React Router's `withRouter` [8] functions are higher-order components: they accept a component, inject some props into it, and return it back.

As you can see, higher-order components are quite complicated to write and understand. So when hooks were introduced, it's no wonder everyone switched to them.

Now, instead of creating complicated mental maps of which prop goes where and trying to figure out how `theme` ended up in props, we can just write:

```
const Button = () => {
  // we see immediately where the theme is coming from
```

```
  const { theme } = useTheme();

  return <button appearance={theme} ...>Button</button>
};
```

Everything that is happening in the component can be read from top to
bottom, and the source of all the data is obvious, which significantly
simplifies debugging and development.

And while hooks have probably replaced 99% of shared logic concerns and
100% of use cases for accessing context, higher-order components can still
be useful even in modern code. Mostly for enhancing callbacks, React
lifecycle events, and intercepting DOM and keyboard events. Only if you're
feeling fancy, of course. Those use cases can also be implemented with
hooks, just not as elegantly.

Let's take a look at them.

Enhancing callbacks

Imagine you need to send some sort of advanced logging on some callbacks.
When you click a button, for example, you want to send some logging
events with some data. How would you do it with hooks? You'd probably
have a `Button` component with an `onClick` callback:

```
const Button = ({ onClick, children }) => {
  return <button onClick={onClick}>{children}</button>;
};
```

And then on the consumer side, you'd hook into that callback and send
logging events there:

```
const SomePage = () => {
  const log = useLoggingSystem();

  const onClick = () => {
    log('Button was clicked');
```

```
    };

    return <Button onClick={onClick}>Click here</Button>;
};
```

And that is fine if you want to fire an event or two. But what if you want
your logging events to be consistently fired across your entire app whenever
the button is clicked? We probably can bake it into the `Button`
component itself:

```
const Button = ({ onClick }) => {
    const log = useLoggingSystem();

    const onButtonClick = () => {
        log('Button was clicked');
        onClick();
    };

    return <button onClick={onButtonClick}>Click me</button>;
};
```

But then what? For proper logs, you'd have to send some sort of data as
well. We surely can extend the `Button` component with some
`loggingData` props and pass it down:

```
const Button = ({ onClick, loggingData }) => {
    const onButtonClick = () => {
        log('Button was clicked', loggingData);
        onClick();
    };
    return <button onClick={onButtonClick}>Click me</button>;
};
```

But what if you want to fire the same events when the click has happened
on other components? `Button` is usually not the only thing people can
click on in our apps. What if I want to add the same logging to a
`ListItem` component? Copy-paste exactly the same logic there?

```
const ListItem = ({ onClick, loggingData }) => {
  const onListItemClick = () => {
    log('List item was clicked', loggingData);
    onClick();
  };
  return <Item onClick={onListItemClick}>Click me</Item>;
};
```

Too much copy-pasting and prone to errors and someone forgetting to change something in my taste.

What I want, essentially, is to encapsulate the logic of "something triggered `onClick` callback - send some logging events" somewhere and then just reuse it in any component I want without changing the code of those components in any way.

This is the first use case where hooks are of no use, but higher-order components could come in handy.

Instead of copy-pasting the "click happened → log data" logic everywhere, I can create a `withLoggingOnClick` function that:

- Accepts a component as an argument.
- Intercepts its `onClick` callback.
- Sends the data that I need to whatever external framework is used for logging.
- Returns the component with the onClick callback intact for further use.

It would look something like this:

```
// just a function that accepts Component as an argument
export const withLoggingOnClick = (Component) => {
  return (props) => {
    const onClick = () => {
      console.log('Log on click something');
      // don't forget to call onClick that is coming from props!
      // we're overriding it below
      props.onClick();
```

```
  };

  // return original component with all the props
  // and overriding onClick with our own callback
  return <Component {...props} onClick={onClick} />;
  };
};
```

Now, I can just add it to **any** component that I want. I can have a `Button` with logging baked in:

```
export const ButtonWithLoggingOnClick =
  withLoggingOnClick(SimpleButton);
```

Or use it in the list item:

```
export const ListItemWithLoggingOnClick =
  withLoggingOnClick(ListItem);
```

Or any other component that has an `onClick` callback that I want to track. Without a single line of code changed in either `Button` or `ListItem` components!

> **Interactive example and full code**
> https://advanced-react.com/examples/07/02

Adding data to the higher-order component

Now, what's left to do is to add some data from the outside to the logging function. Considering that a higher-order component is nothing more than just a function, we can do that easily. We just need to add some other arguments to the function, that's it:

```
export const withLoggingOnClickWithParams = (
  Component,
  // adding some params as a second argument to the function
```

```
      params,
    ) => {
      return (props) => {
        const onClick = () => {
          // accessing params that we passed as an argument here
          // everything else stays the same
          console.log('Log on click: ', params.text);
          props.onClick();
        };

        return <Component {...props} onClick={onClick} />;
      };
    };
```

Now, when we wrap our button with a higher-order component, we can pass the text that we want to log:

```
const ButtonWithLoggingOnClickWithParams =
  withLoggingOnClickWithParams(SimpleButton, {
    text: 'button component',
  });
```

On the consumer side, we'd just use this button as a normal button component, without worrying about the logging text:

```
const Page = () => {
  return (
    <ButtonWithLoggingOnClickWithParams
      onClick={onClickCallback}
    >
      Click me
    </ButtonWithLoggingOnClickWithParams>
  );
};
```

But what if we actually **want** to worry about this text? What if we want to send different texts in different contexts of where the button is used? We wouldn't want to create a million wrapped buttons for every use case.

Also very easy to solve: instead of passing that text as a function's argument, we can just pass it as a prop to the resulting button. The code would look like this:

```
<ButtonWithLoggingOnClickWithProps
  onClick={onClickCallback}
  logText="this is Page button"
>
  Click me
</ButtonWithLoggingOnClickWithProps>
```

And then we can just extract that `logText` from props that were sent to the button:

```
export const withLoggingOnClickWithProps = (Component) => {
  // it will be in the props here, just extract it
  return ({ logText, ...props }) => {
    const onClick = () => {
      // and then just use it here
      console.log('Log on click: ', logText);
      props.onClick();
    };

    return <Component {...props} onClick={onClick} />;
  };
};
```

Interactive example and full code
https://advanced-react.com/examples/07/03

Enhancing React lifecycle events

We are not limited to clicks and callbacks here. Remember, these are just components, we can do whatever we want and need. We can use everything React has to offer. For example, we can send those logging events when a component is mounted:

```
export const withLoggingOnMount = (Component) => {
  return (props) => {
    // no more overriding onClick
    // use normal useEffect - it's just a component!
    useEffect(() => {
      console.log('log on mount');
    }, []);

    // and pass back props intact
    return <Component {...props} />;
  };
};
```

or even read props and send them on re-renders, when a certain prop has changed:

```
export const withLoggingOnReRender = (Component) => {
  return ({ id, ...props }) => {
    // fire logging every time "id" prop changes
    useEffect(() => {
      console.log('log on id change');
    }, [id]);

    // and pass back props intact
    return <Component {...props} />;
  };
};
```

> **Interactive example and full code**
> https://advanced-react.com/examples/07/04

Intercepting DOM events

Another very useful application of higher-order components is intercepting various DOM and keyboard events. Imagine, for example, you're implementing some sort of keyboard shortcuts functionality for your page.

When specific keys are pressed, you want to do various things, like opening dialogs, creating issues, etc. You'd probably add an event listener to the window for something like this:

```
useEffect(() => {
  const keyPressListener = (event) => {
    // do stuff
  };

  window.addEventListener('keypress', keyPressListener);

  return () =>
    window.removeEventListener(
      'keypress',
      keyPressListener,
    );
}, []);
```

And then, you have various parts of your app, like modal dialogs, dropdown menus, drawers, etc., where you want to block that global listener while the dialog is open. If it was just one dialog, you could manually add `onKeyPress` to the dialog itself and there do `event.stopPropagation()` for that:

```
export const Modal = ({ onClose }) => {
  const onKeyPress = (event) => event.stopPropagation();

  return (
    <div onKeyPress={onKeyPress}>...// dialog code</div>
  );
};
```

But the same story as with `onClick` logging - what if you have multiple components where you want to see this logic? Copy-paste that `event.stopPropagation` everywhere? Meh.

What we can do instead is, again, implement a higher-order component. This time it will accept a component, wrap it in a div with `onKeyPress` callback attached, and return the component unchanged.

```
export const withSuppressKeyPress = (Component) => {
  return (props) => {
    const onKeyPress = (event) => {
      event.stopPropagation();
    };

    return (
      <div onKeyPress={onKeyPress}>
        <Component {...props} />
      </div>
    );
  };
};
```

That is it! Now we can wrap any component in it:

```
const ModalWithSuppressedKeyPress =
  withSuppressKeyPress(Modal);
const DropdownWithSuppressedKeyPress =
  withSuppressKeyPress(Dropdown);
// etc
```

and just use it everywhere:

```
const Component = () => {
  return <ModalWithSuppressedKeyPress />;
};
```

Now, when this modal is open and focused, any key press event will bubble up through the elements' hierarchy until it reaches our `div` in `withSuppressKeyPress` that wraps the modal and will stop there. Mission accomplished, and developers who implement the `Modal` component don't even need to know or care about it.

Interactive example and full code
https://advanced-react.com/examples/07/05

Key takeaways

That's enough of a history lesson for the book, I think. A few things to remember before we jump to the next chapter, with the most exciting and the most controversial part of React: state management!

- A higher-order component is just a function that accepts a component as an argument and returns a new component. That new component renders the component from the argument.
- We can inject props or additional logic into the components that are wrapped in a higher-order component.

```javascript
// accept a Component as an argument
const withSomeLogic = (Component) => {
  // inject some logic here

  // return a component that renders the component from the argument
  // inject some prop to it
  return (props) => {
    // or inject some logic here
    // can use React hooks here, it's just a component

    return <Component {...props} some="data" />;
  };
};
```

- We can pass additional data to the higher-order component, either through the function's argument or through props.

Chapter 8. React Context and performance

One final and very important piece of the "re-renders in React" puzzle is Context. Context has a bad reputation when it comes to re-renders. I have a feeling, that sometimes people treat Context as an evil gremlin that just roams around the app, causing spontaneous and unstoppable re-renders just because it can. As a result, developers sometimes try to avoid using Context at all costs.

Part of this reputation is deserved, of course: Context has its issues. However, what is often underestimated or not known at all is that Context can prevent unnecessary re-renders and significantly improve the performance of our apps as a result. When applied correctly and carefully, of course.

But most importantly, understanding Context is very useful when it comes to external state management libraries like Redux. The mental model is exactly the same. If you learn Context, you'll be able to use any state management library out there in the most optimal way with very little effort.

So let's implement an app with and without Context, explore the possibilities, and in the process learn:

- The kind of performance improvement Context can offer.
- The caveats of using Context.
- How to get the most out of Context and prevent unnecessary re-renders caused by it.

The problem

Imagine you were implementing a page with a two-column layout: a sidebar on the left and the "main" part on the right. The left sidebar needs to be collapsible: it should have a button, a click on which will collapse the sidebar into the "narrow" view or expand it back to the "wide" view. As a result, the main part can also become bigger or smaller. And somewhere at the bottom of that main part, you have a block where you want to show something in three columns when the sidebar is collapsed or in two columns when it's expanded. Maybe an image gallery or some advertisement blocks.

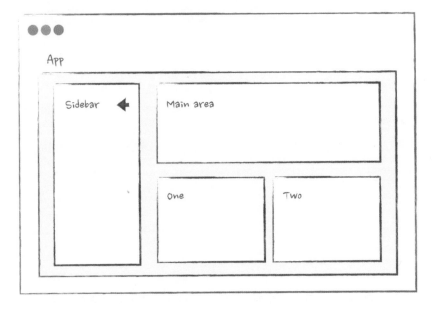

From the code perspective, the app looks something like this. It would have a `Page` component that assembles the entire app together:

```
const Page = () => {
  return (
    <Layout>
      <Sidebar />
      <MainPart />
    </Layout>
  );
};
```

`Sidebar` component that renders a bunch of links, plugins, menus, etc., and the "expand/collapse" button:

```
const Sidebar = () => {
  return (
    <div className="sidebar">
      {/* this one will control the expand/collapse */}
      <ExpandButton />

      {/* ... other sidebar stuff */}
      <Link ... />
      <Plugin ... />
    </div>
  )
}
```

And the `MainPart` component, which renders lots of slow stuff, and somewhere at the bottom, it has that block that will render two or three columns, depending on whether the `Sidebar` is expanded or collapsed:

```
const MainPart = () => {
  return (
    <>
      <VerySlowComponent />
      <AnotherVerySlowComponent />
      {/* this one needs to know whether the sidebar is expanded or
collapsed */}
      {/* it will render two or three columns, depending on this
information */}
      <AdjustableColumnsBlock />
    </>
  );
};
```

And now, how would we implement the expand/collapse behavior? We'd have to introduce some `isNavExpanded` state and hold that information there. And both `ExpandButton` in the `Sidebar` component and `AdjustableColumnsBlock` in the `MainPart` need to have access to it. Considering this, if we were implementing this naively, we'd have no choice

but to store that state at the closest parent of both of those components:
`Page` .

```
const Page = () => {
  const [isNavExpanded, setIsNavExpanded] = useState();

  return ...
}
```

And then pass the set function and the state itself through props of the
`Sidebar` and `MainPart` components to `ExpandButton` :

```
const Sidebar = ({ isNavExpanded, toggleNav }) => {
  return (
    <div className="sidebar">
      {/* pass the props here */}
      <ExpandButton
        isExpanded={isNavExpanded}
        onClick={toggleNav}
      />
      {/* ... // the rest of the stuff */}
    </div>
  );
};
```

and `AdjustableColumnsBlock` :

```
const MainPart = ({ isNavExpanded }) => {
  return (
    <>
      <VerySlowComponent />
      <AnotherVerySlowComponent />
      <AdjustableColumnsBlock
        isNavExpanded={isNavExpanded}
      />
    </>
  );
};
```

The full code of the `Page` component will look like this then:

```
const Page = () => {
  const [isNavExpanded, setIsNavExpanded] = useState();

  return (
    <Layout>
      <Sidebar
        isNavExpanded={isNavExpanded}
        toggleNav={() => setIsNavExpanded(!isNavExpanded)}
      />
      <MainPart isNavExpanded={isNavExpanded} />
    </Layout>
  );
};
```

While technically, it will work, it's not the best solution. Firstly, our `Sidebar` and `MainPart` now have props that they don't use but merely pass to the components below - their API becomes bloated and harder to read.

And secondly, performance will be pretty bad. What will happen here from the re-renders perspective? Every time the button is clicked, and navigation is expanded/collapsed, the state in the `Page` component will change. And as we know from *Chapter 1. Intro to re-renders*, state update will cause this component and every component inside, including their children, to re-render. Both `Sidebar` and `MainPart` have a lot of components, some of which are quite slow. So re-rendering of the entire page will be slow, making navigation expanding/collapsing slow and laggy as a result.

Interactive example and full code
https://advanced-react.com/examples/08/01

And unfortunately, we can't just use any of the composition techniques from the previous chapters to prevent this: all of them actually depend on the state that causes re-rendering. We can probably memoize the intermediate slow components that don't depend on that state. But the code of that will become even more bloated: all of them would have to be memoized!

There is a better way: Context.

How Context can help

In situations like this, Context (or any context-like state management library) is very powerful. What they allow us to do is escape that tree of components and, instead of passing data through props, we can pass it directly from the component at the very top to the component at the bottom.

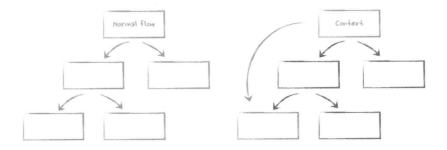

It would work like this. We can extract the expand/collapse functionality from the `Page` component away. The state and the `toggle` function, nothing else:

```
const NavigationController = () => {
  const [isNavExpanded, setIsNavExpanded] = useState();

  const toggle = () => setIsNavExpanded(!isNavExpanded);
};
```

Then, we pass everything that is supposed to render on the `Page` as `children` (we discussed this pattern in detail in *Chapter 2. Elements, children as props, and re-renders*):

```
const NavigationController = ({ children }) => {
```

```
const [isNavExpanded, setIsNavExpanded] = useState();

const toggle = () => setIsNavExpanded(!isNavExpanded);

return children;
};
```

This is the "children as props" pattern. Our `Page` then uses that controller on top of everything else:

```
const Page = () => {
  return (
    <NavigationController>
      <Layout>
        <Sidebar />
        <MainPart />
      </Layout>
    </NavigationController>
  );
};
```

All props will disappear, and most importantly, none of the components in the Page, like `Layout` or `Sidebar`, will be affected by the state change inside `NavigationController`. As covered in *Chapter 2. Elements, children as props, and re-renders*, `children` when passed like this are nothing more than props, and props are not affected by state changes.

Finally, we introduce Context in the `NavigationController`, which will hold the navigation state and API to change that state (i.e., the `toggle` function):

```
// creating context with default values
const Context = React.createContext({
  isNavExpanded: true,
  toggle: () => {},
});
```

Render that Context provider inside the `NavigationController`:

```
const NavigationController = ({ children }) => {
  const [isNavExpanded, setIsNavExpanded] = useState();

  const toggle = () => setIsNavExpanded(!isNavExpanded);

  return <Context.Provider>{children}</Context.Provider>;
};
```

And finally, the step that will make it work: we pass the `value` property to this Context. Just an object that includes the `isNavExpanded` state value and the `toggle` function.

```
const NavigationController = ({ children }) => {
  const [isNavExpanded, setIsNavExpanded] = useState();

  const toggle = () => setIsNavExpanded(!isNavExpanded);

  const value = { isNavExpanded, toggle };

  return (
    <Context.Provider value={value}>
      {children}
    </Context.Provider>
  );
};
```

Now every component that happens to be rendered down the tree from that provider (even if they are passed as props like our `children` !) will now have access to that `value` through the `useContext` hook.

We can introduce a nice `useNavigation` hook:

```
// pass that Context to the useContext hook
const useNavigation = () => useContext(Context);
```

And then use that hook to gain access to the state *directly* in those components that actually need this information. We'll use it in the expand/collapse button itself:

```
const ExpandButton = () => {
  const { isNavExpanded, toggle } = useNavigation();

  return (
    <button onClick={toggle}>
      {isNavExpanded ? 'Collapse' : 'Expand'}
    </button>
  );
};
```

And directly in the block where we want to render the different number of columns based on the navigation state:

```
const AdjustableColumnsBlock = () => {
  const { isNavExpanded } = useNavigation();

  return isNavExpanded ? <TwoColumns /> : <ThreeColumns />;
};
```

No more passing props around anywhere! Now, when the state changes, the `value` prop on the Context provider will change, and only components that use the `useNavigation` hook will re-render. All other components inside `Sidebar` or `MainBlock` don't use it, so they will be safe and won't re-render. Just like that, with the simple use of Context, we've drastically improved the performance of the entire app.

> **Interactive example and full code**
> https://advanced-react.com/examples/08/02

It's not all sunshine and roses when dealing with Context, of course. Otherwise, it wouldn't have such a bad reputation. There are three major things that you need to know like the back of your hand when introducing Context into the app:

- Context consumers will re-render when the `value` on the `Provider` changes.

- **All** of them will re-render, even if they don't use the part of the `value` that actually changed.
- Those re-renders can't be prevented with memoization (easily).

Let's take a closer look at these and how to mitigate them.

Context value change

Every time the `value` prop on the Context provider changes, everyone who uses this Context will re-render.

Let's take a look at our Context code again:

```
const NavigationController = ({ children }) => {
  const [isNavExpanded, setIsNavExpanded] = useState();

  const toggle = () => setIsNavExpanded(!isNavExpanded);

  const value = { isNavExpanded, toggle };

  return (
    <Context.Provider value={value}>
      {children}
    </Context.Provider>
  );
};

const useNavigation = () => useContext(Context);
```

Every time we change state, the `value` object changes, so every component that uses this Context through `useNavigation` will re-render. This is natural and expected: we want everyone to have access to the latest value, and the only way in React to update components is to re-render them.

However, what will happen if the `NavigationController` re-renders for any other reason other than its own state change? If, for example, this re-render is triggered in its parent component?

`NavigationController` will also re-render: it's React's natural chain of re-renders. The `value` object will be re-created, and we're again in the situation where React needs to compare objects between re-renders. The referential equality problem kicks in yet again (we've covered it in detail in *Chapter 6. Deep dive into diffing and reconciliation*). As a result, the `value` that we pass to the provider will change, and every single component that uses this Context will re-render for no reason.

In the case of our small app, it's not a problem: the provider sits at the very top, so nothing above it can re-render. However, this won't always be the case. And in large, complicated apps, it's more likely than not that someone will introduce something one day that triggers the re-render of that provider.

For example, in our `Page` component, I might decide one day to move that provider inside the `Layout` component to simplify the `Page`:

```
const Page = () => {
  return (
    <Layout>
      <Sidebar />
      <MainPart />
    </Layout>
  );
};
```

and `Layout` will render the context now:

```
const Layout = ({ children }) => {
  return (
    <NavigationController>
      <div className="layout">{children}</div>
    </NavigationController>
  );
};
```

Everything still works perfectly as before, just with slightly cleaner composition. But what will happen if I introduce some state into that

Layout ? Maybe I want to track scrolling on the page there:

```
const Layout = ({ children }) => {
  const [scroll, setScroll] = useState();

  useEffect(() => {
    window.addEventListener('scroll', () => {
      setScroll(window.scrollY);
    });
  }, []);

  return (
    <NavigationController>
      <div className="layout">{children}</div>
    </NavigationController>
  );
};
```

Normally, this wouldn't be a problem: this is the "children as props" pattern, the state is limited to the `Layout` only, and no one else on the `Page` is affected.

But in this case, the `NavigationController` component is also rendered inside. So the state change on scroll will cause it to re-render, the `value` in the provider will change, and all components that use that Context will re-render.

And if that Context is used in a heavy component or in a component with a lot of children, then - oops, half of the app re-renders on every scroll, and everything becomes super slow.

Interactive example and full code
https://advanced-react.com/examples/08/03

Fortunately, all of this is easily preventable. We just need to use `useMemo` and `useCallback` to memoize the value passed to the provider:

```
const NavigationController = ({ children }) => {
```

```
const [isNavExpanded, setIsNavExpanded] = useState();

const toggle = useCallback(() => {
  setIsNavExpanded(!isNavExpanded);
}, [isNavExpanded]);

const value = useMemo(() => {
  return { isNavExpanded, toggle };
}, [isNavExpanded, toggle]);

return (
  <Context.Provider value={value}>
    {children}
  </Context.Provider>
);
};
```

Interactive example and full code
https://advanced-react.com/examples/08/04

This is one of the few cases where always memoizing by default is actually not premature optimization. It will prevent much bigger problems in the future that will almost inevitably occur.

Preventing unnecessary Context re-renders: split providers

On top of the fact that all context consumers re-render when the value changes, it's important to emphasize not only the "value changes" part but also that **all** of them will do that. If I introduce `open` and `close` functions to our navigation API that don't actually depend on the state:

```
const SomeComponent = () => {
  // no dependencies, open won't change
  const open = useCallback(() => setIsNavExpanded(true), []);
```

```
  // no dependencies, close won't change
  const close = useCallback(() => setIsNavExpanded(false), []);

  const value = useMemo(() => {
    return { isNavExpanded, open, close };
  }, [isNavExpanded, open, close]);

  return ...
}
```

And try using one of them somewhere:

```
const SomeComponent = () => {
  const { open } = useNavigation();

  return ...
}
```

The `SomeComponent` will re-render when the `value` on the Context
provider changes, despite the fact that the `open` function doesn't actually
change.

And no amount of memoization will prevent it. This, for example, won't
work:

```
const useNavOpen = () => {
  const { open } = useNavigation();

  return useCallback(open, []);
};
```

We can, however, use an interesting technique called "splitting providers"
to achieve the desired result.

It works like this. Instead of just one Context that holds everything, we can
create two: one will hold the value that changes, and another one will hold
those that don't.

```
// store the state here
```

```
const ContextData = React.createContext({
  isNavExpanded: false,
});
// store the open/close functions here
const ContextApi = React.createContext({
  open: () => {},
  close: () => {},
});
```

And instead of just one provider in the `NavigationController`, we'll render two:

```
const NavigationController = ({ children }) => {
  ...

  return (
    <ContextData.Provider value={data}>
      <ContextApi.Provider value={api}>
        {children}
      </ContextApi.Provider>
    </ContextData.Provider>
  )
}
```

The values that we pass to those providers will be the `data` that has the state and `api` that only holds references to `open` and `close` functions.

```
const NavigationController = ({ children }) => {
  ...

  // that one has a dependency on state
  const data = useMemo(() => ({ isNavExpanded }), [isNavExpanded]);

  // that one never changes - no dependencies
  const api = useMemo(() => ({ open, close }), [close, open]);

  return (
    <ContextData.Provider value={data}>
      <ContextApi.Provider value={api}>
        {children}
```

```
      </ContextApi.Provider>
    </ContextData.Provider>
  )
}
```

We'd have to drop the `toggle` function here, unfortunately. It depends on the state, so we can't put it into the `api` , and it doesn't really make sense to include it in the data.

Now, we just need to introduce two hooks to abstract away the context:

```
const useNavigationData = () => useContext(ContextData);
const useNavigationApi = () => useContext(ContextApi);
```

Then, in our `SomeComponent` , we can use the `open` function freely. It will trigger expand/collapse as intended, but `SomeComponent` won't re-render because of it:

```
const SomeComponent = () => {
  const { open } = useNavigationApi();

  return ...
}
```

Where we previously used the `useNavigation` hook to get the `isNavExpanded` value, we'll now use `useNavigationData` , without changing anything else:

```
const AdjustableColumnsBlock = () => {
  const { isNavExpanded } = useNavigationData();

  return isNavExpanded ? <TwoColumns /> : <ThreeColumns />;
};
```

Interactive example and full code
https://advanced-react.com/examples/08/05

Of course, we can split these providers as granularly as we need. It depends solely on what makes sense for your application and whether re-renders because of Context are actually harmful.

Reducers and split providers

As you probably noticed above, I had to drop the `toggle` function from our app. Unfortunately, the `toggle` depends on the state, so if I added it to the `api` provider, it would start depending on the state as well, and the split wouldn't make sense anymore:

```
const NavigationController = ({ children }) => {
  ...
  // depends on isNavExpanded
  const toggle = useCallback(() => setIsNavExpanded(!isNavExpanded),
[isNavExpanded]);

  // with toggle it has to depend on isNavExpanded through toggle
function
  // so will change with every state update
  const api = useMemo(() => ({ open, close, toggle }), [open, close,
toggle]);

  return (
    <ContextData.Provider value={data}>
      <ContextApi.Provider value={api}>
        {children}
      </ContextApi.Provider>
    </ContextData.Provider>
  )
```

This isn't ideal, though. Now, anyone who tries to use that state would have to implement that toggle functionality themselves:

```
const ExpandButton = () => {
  const { isNavExpanded, open, close } = useNavigation();

  return (
```

```
    <button onClick={isNavExpanded ? close : open}>
      {isNavExpanded ? 'Collapse' : 'Expand'}
    </button>
  );
};
```

This doesn't make much sense. Ideally, the navigation's API should be able to handle common cases like this by itself.

And it can! All we need is to switch our regular state management from `useState` hook to `useReducer`.

`useReducer` is a different way to manage a component's state. Instead of being aware of the state we're changing and manipulating it manually, the reducers pattern allows us just to dispatch named "actions". This is usually very convenient when you have a complicated state or complex operations on that state, and you want a more structured approach to managing them.

In our case, it would look something like this. Instead of our `isNavExpanded` state and `open`, `close`, and `toggle` functions that manually change that state:

```
const [isNavExpanded, setIsNavExpanded] = useState();

const toggle = () => setIsNavExpanded(!isNavExpanded);
const open = () => setIsNavExpanded(true);
const close = () => setIsNavExpanded(false);
```

We'll introduce a reducer:

```
const [state, dispatch] = useReducer(reducer, {
  isNavExpanded: true,
});
```

And declare our functions like this:

```
const toggle = () => dispatch({ type: 'toggle-sidebar' });
const open = () => dispatch({ type: 'open-sidebar' });
const close = () => dispatch({ type: 'close-sidebar' });
```

Notice how none of the functions depend on the state anymore, including the `toggle`. All they do is dispatch an action.

Then, we'd introduce the reducer function, inside of which we'll perform all the state manipulations for all of our actions. The `reducer` function controls and changes that state. The function accepts the state it needs to transform and the "actions" value: the value that we use in the `dispatch` above.

```
const reducer = (state, action) => {
  ...
}
```

To implement it, we'll use a simple `switch/case` operation:

```
const reducer = (state, action) => {
  switch (action.type) {
    case 'open-sidebar':
      return { ...state, isNavExpanded: true };
    case 'close-sidebar':
      return { ...state, isNavExpanded: false };
    case 'toggle-sidebar':
      // we'll have access to the old value here - it's our "state"
      // so just flip it around
      return {
        ...state,
        isNavExpanded: !state.isNavExpanded,
      };
  }
};
```

Now all we have to do is add these functions to our api:

```
const NavigationController = () => {
  // state and dispatch are returned from the useReducer
  const [state, dispatch] = useReducer(reducer, { ... });

  const api = useMemo(() => {
```

```
    return {
      open: () => dispatch({ type: 'open-sidebar' }),
      close: () => dispatch({ type: 'close-sidebar' }),
      toggle: () => dispatch({ type: 'toggle-sidebar' }),
    }
    // don't depend on the state directly anymore!
  }, []);
}
```

And now, when we pass that `api` value to the provider, none of the
consumers of that Context will re-render on state change: the `value`
never changes! And we can safely use the `toggle` function everywhere,
without the fear of causing performance problems in the app.

Interactive example and full code
https://advanced-react.com/examples/08/06

This reducer pattern is especially powerful when you have multiple state
variables and more complex actions to perform on the state, rather than
just flipping a boolean from `false` to `true` . But from the re-render
perspective, it's the same as `useState` : updating the state through
`dispatch` will force the component to re-render.

Context selectors

But what if you don't want to migrate your state to reducers or split
providers? What if you only need to occasionally use one of the values from
Context in a performance-sensitive area, and the rest of the app is fine? If I
want to close my navigation and force the page to go into full-screen mode
when I focus on some heavy editor component, for example? Splitting
providers and going with reducers seems too extreme of a change just to be
able to use the `open` function from Context without re-renders once.

In something like Redux, we'd use memoized state selectors in this case.
Unfortunately, for Context, this won't work - any change in context value

will trigger the re-render of every consumer.

```
const useOpen = () => {
  const { open } = useContext(Context);

  // even if we additionally memoize it here, it won't help
  // change in Context value will trigger re-render of the component
  that uses useOpen
  return useMemo(() => open, []);
};
```

There is, however, a trick that can mimic the desired behavior and allow us to select a value from Context that doesn't cause the component to re-render. We can leverage the power of Higher Order Components for this!

The trick is this. First, we'll create a `withNavigationOpen` higher-order component:

```
// it's a HOC, so it accepts a component and returns another component
const withNavigationOpen = (AnyComponent) => {
  return (props) => <AnyComponent {...props} />;
};
```

Second, we'll use our Context to extract the `open` function from the provider and pass it as a prop to the component from the arguments:

```
const withNavigationOpen = (AnyComponent) => {
  return (props) => {
    // access Context here - it's just another component
    const { open } = useContext(Context);

    return <AnyComponent {...props} openNav={open} />;
  };
};
```

Now, every component that is wrapped in that HOC will have the `openNav` prop:

```
// openNav is coming from HOC
const SomeHeavyComponent = withNavigationOpen(
  ({ openNav }) => {
    return <button onClick={openNav} />;
  },
);
```

But that doesn't solve anything yet: the heavy component will still re-render every time the Context value changes. We need the final step here: memoize the component we passed as an argument inside the HOC itself:

```
const withNavigationOpen = (AnyComponent) => {
  // wrap the component from the arguments in React.memo here
  const AnyComponentMemo = React.memo(AnyComponent);

  return (props) => {
    const { open } = useContext(Context);

    // return memoized component here
    // now it won't re-render because of Context changes
    // make sure that whatever is passed as props here don't change
between re-renders!
    return <AnyComponentMemo {...props} openNav={open} />;
  };
};
```

Now, when the Context value changes, the component that uses anything from Context will still re-render: our *unnamed component* that we return from the `withNavigationOpen` function. But this component renders another component that is *memoized*. So if its props don't change, it won't re-render because of this re-render. And the props won't change: those that are spread are coming from "outside", so they won't be affected by the context change. And the `open` function is memoized inside the Context provider itself.

Our `SomeHeavyComponent` can safely use the `openNav` function: it won't re-render when the Context value changes.

Key takeaways

I hope this chapter has given you an idea of how useful Context can be when it comes to re-renders. And for reducing props on components, for that matter. I'm not advocating for using Context everywhere, of course: its caveats are pretty serious. So for larger, more complex apps, it's probably better to go with an external state management solution right away. Any solution that supports memoized selectors. But it could work for smaller apps, where you have just a few places that could benefit from the Context mental model.

And don't forget:

- With Context (or any context-like state management library), we can pass data directly from one component to another deep in the render tree without the need to wire it through props.
- Passing data in this way can improve the performance of our apps, as we'll avoid the re-rendering of all components in between.
- Context, however, can be dangerous: all components that use it will re-render if the value in the Context provider changes. This re-render can't be stopped with standard memoization techniques.
- To minimize Context re-renders, we should always memoize the value we pass to the provider.
- We can split the Context provider into multiple providers to further minimize re-renders. Switching from useState to useReducer can help with this.
- Even though we don't have proper selectors for Context, we can imitate their functionality with higher order components and React.memo.

Chapter 9. Refs: from storing data to imperative API

One of the many beautiful things about React is that it abstracts away the complexity of dealing with the real DOM. Instead of manually querying elements, scratching our heads over how to add classes to those elements, or struggling with browser inconsistencies, we can just write components and focus on the user experience now. There are, however, still cases (very few though!) when we need to get access to the actual DOM.

To do that, we need Refs. No mysteries this time, let's just implement a fancy form with simple validation of the input field. In the process, we'll learn:

- Why we still need access to DOM elements.
- What Ref is, and what the difference is between Refs and state.
- How to use Refs to get access to UI elements.
- What `forwardRef` is, how to use it, and how to avoid using it (you'll see why!)
- Why we still need imperative APIs in React, and how to implement them with or without `useImperativeHandle`.

Accessing the DOM in React

Let's say I want to implement a sign-up form for a conference I'm organizing. I want people to give me their name, email, and Twitter handle before I can send them the details. "Name" and "email" fields I want to make mandatory. But I don't want to show some annoying red borders around those inputs when people try to submit them empty. I want the form to be cool. So instead, I want to focus the empty field and shake it a little to attract attention, just for the fun of it.

Now, React gives us a lot, but it doesn't give us *everything*. Things like "focus an element manually" or "shake that element" are not part of the package. For that, we need to dust off our rusty native JavaScript API skills. And for that, we need access to the actual DOM element.

In the non-React world, we'd do something like this:

```
const element = document.getElementById('bla');
```

After that, we can focus it:

```
element.focus();
```

Or scroll to it:

```
element.scrollIntoView();
```

Or anything else our heart desires. Some typical use cases for using the native DOM API in the React world would include:

- Manually **focusing an element** after it's rendered, like an input field in a form.
- Detecting **a click outside of a component** when showing popup-like elements.
- Manually **scrolling to an element** after it appears on the screen.
- **Calculating sizes and boundaries** of components on the screen to correctly position something like a tooltip.

And although, technically, nothing is stopping us from doing `getElementById` even today, React gives us a slightly more powerful way to access that element that doesn't require us to spread ids everywhere or be aware of the underlying DOM structure: Refs.

What is Ref?

A Ref is a mutable object that React preserves between re-renders. Remember that everything declared within a component will be re-created all the time?

```
const Component = () => {
  // "data" object will be new with every re-render
  const data = { id: 'test' };
};
```

Components are just functions, so everything inside is basically a local variable to that function. Refs allow us to bypass that limitation.

To create a Ref, we can use the `useRef` hook with the Ref's initial value passed to it:

```
const Component = () => {
  const ref = useRef({ id: 'test' });
};
```

That initial value will now be available via the `ref.current` property: everything that we pass to the Ref is stored there.

```
const Component = () => {
  // pass initial value here
  const ref = useRef({ id: 'test' });

  useEffect(() => {
    // access it here
    console.log(ref.current);
  });
};
```

The initial value is cached, so if we compare `ref.current` between re-renders, the reference will be the same. It's the same as if we'd just used the `useMemo` hook on that object.

Once that Ref is created, we can assign anything to it within `useEffect` or event handlers. It's just an object, nothing special:

```
const Component = () => {
  useEffect(() => {
    // assign url as an id, when it changes
    ref.current = { id: url };
  }, [url]);
};
```

And all of this looks awfully similar to the state, isn't it? Just the API is different. What's the catch, then? Why do we use state everywhere, but Ref is considered an escape hatch that should not be used? Let's figure this out first before making our form too fancy. Maybe we don't need the state there at all?

Difference between Ref and state

Let's start with the form and implement the first input field with the submit button.

```
const Form = () => {
  return (
    <>
      <input type="text" />
      <button onClick={submit}>submit</button>
    </>
  );
};
```

Now, in order for our submit to work, we need to extract the input field content somehow. In React, normally, we'd just add an `onChange` callback to the `input`, save that information in the state so that it's preserved between re-renders, and then access it in the `submit` function:

```
const Form = () => {
  const [value, setValue] = useState();

  const onChange = (e) => {
    setValue(e.target.value);
```

```
  };
  const submit = () => {
    // send to the backend here
    console.log(value);
  };

  return (
    <>
      <input type="text" onChange={onChange} />
      <button onClick={submit}>submit</button>
    </>
  );
};
```

But I mentioned a few times already that whatever we store in a Ref is also preserved between re-renders. And, conveniently, anything can be assigned to a Ref. What will happen if I just save the value from the input there instead of the state?

```
const Form = () => {
  const ref = useRef();

  const onChange = (e) => {
    // save it to ref instead of state
    ref.current = e.target.value;
  };
  const submit = () => {
    // get it from ref instead of state
    console.log(ref.current);
  };

  return (
    <>
      <input type="text" onChange={onChange} />
      <button onClick={submit}>submit</button>
    </>
  );
};
```

It seems to work exactly as with state: I type something in the input field, then press the button, and the value is sent.

Interactive example and full code
https://advanced-react.com/examples/09/01

So what's the difference? And why we don't usually see this pattern in our apps? A few reasons for this.

Ref update doesn't trigger re-render

One of the biggest and most visible differences between Refs and state is that Refs update don't cause re-renders. If you put `console.log` in both of those forms, you'll see that the `Form` component with the state re-renders with every keystroke, while the `Form` with the Ref stays quiet.

```
useEffect(() => {
  console.log('Form component re-renders');
});
```

On the surface, this seems like great news. Isn't like half of this book dedicated to re-renders and how to escape them? If Refs don't cause re-renders, surely they are the solution to all our performance problems?

Not at all. If you remember from the first chapter, re-render is a crucial piece of the React lifecycle. This is how React updates our components with new information. If, for example, I want to show the number of letters typed into the text field under the field, I can't do this with Refs.

```
const Form = () => {
  const ref = useRef();
  const numberOfLetters = ref.current?.length ?? 0;

  return (
    <>
```

```
      <input type="text" onChange={onChange} />
      {/* Not going to work */}
      Characters count: {numberOfLetters}
      <button onClick={submit}>submit</button>
    </>
  );
};
```

Refs update doesn't cause re-renders, so our `return` output will always show 0 for `numberOfLetters`.

Even more interesting than 0, actually. If something completely unrelated to that input causes the Form component to re-render, the value will suddenly be updated to the latest one. Ref stores that value between re-renders remember? If I add something like a simple modal dialog to that form, then the opening of the dialog will be the trigger that forces the component to update itself and for the number of letters to change.

```
const Form = () => {
  // state for the dialog
  const [isOpen, setIsOpen] = useState(false);
  const ref = useRef();
  const numberOfLetters = ref.current?.length ?? 0;

  return (
    <>
      <input type="text" onChange={onChange} />
      {/* This will not change when you type in the field */}
      {/* Only when you open/close the dialog */}
      Characters count: {numberOfLetters}
      <button onClick={submit}>submit</button>
      {/* Adding dialog here */}
      <button onClick={() => setIsOpen(true)}>
        Open dialog
      </button>
      {isOpen ? <ModalDialog onClose={() => setIsOpen(false)} /> :
null}
    </>
  );
};
```

Interactive example and full code
https://advanced-react.com/examples/09/02

It gets even *more* interesting than that. That change in value will not be picked up by the downstream components if passed as props as a primitive value either.

Imagine, I wanted to implement some sort of "search results" component. It would accept that text value as a prop and show async search results when the user presses the "show results" button:

```
const SearchResults = ({ search }) => {
  const [showResults, setShowResults] = useState(false);

  return (
    <>
      Searching for: {search} <br />
      {/*This will trigger re-render*/}
      <button onClick={() => setShowResults(!showResults)}>
        show results
      </button>
    </>
  );
};
```

If I use that component in our `Form` where we saved the value in Ref, it just won't work.

```
const Form = () => {
  const ref = useRef();

  const onChange = (e) => {
    ref.current = e.target.value;
  };

  return (
    <>
      <input type="text" onChange={onChange} />
      {/* will never be updated */}
```

Page 159

```
      <SearchResults search={ref.current} />
    </>
  );
};
```

Ref update never triggers a re-render, so the `search` prop on the `SearchResults` component is never explicitly updated. Even when we trigger a re-render inside `SearchResults` by clicking the "show results" button, the `search` value remains an empty string.

Interactive example and full code
https://advanced-react.com/examples/09/03

Ref update is synchronous and mutable

And the second big difference is that Ref updates are synchronous. We are just mutating an object after all, which is a synchronous operation in JavaScript. State, however, is typically asynchronous. It's even more than asynchronous: state updates are run in "snapshots". React has a complicated system that manages it and makes sure that the data and components within one "snapshot" are consistent and updated properly. Ref, however, has none of that: we're modifying an object directly, and that's all there is to it.

It becomes very visible when you try to access state and ref values in the `onChange` callback after setting both of them.

```
const Form = () => {
  const [value, setValue] = useState();

  const onChange = (e) => {
    console.log('before', value);
    setValue(e.target.value);
    console.log('after', value); // same as before
  };
```

```
  };
```

Both "before" and "after" values in the code above will be the same. When we call `setValue`, we're not updating the state right away. We're just letting React know that it needs to schedule a state update with the new data after it's done with whatever it's doing now.

With Ref, it's the opposite:

```
const Form = () => {
  const ref = useRef();

  const onChange = (e) => {
    console.log('before', ref.current);
    ref.current = e.target.value;
    console.log('after', ref.current); // already changed
  };
};
```

We modified an object, the data in that object is available right away, but nothing from the React lifecycle is triggered.

When can we use Ref then?

So, considering these differences, when is it actually okay to use Ref to store something, and when is state preferred? Ask yourself these questions:

- Is this value used for rendering components, now or in the future?
- Is this value passed as props to other components in any way, now or in the future?

If the answer to both of these questions is "nope", then Ref is okay to use.

We can use Ref, for example, to store some "dev" information about components. Maybe we're interested in counting how many times a component renders:

```
useEffect(() => {
  ref.current = ref.current + 1;

  console.log('Render number', ref.current);
});
```

Or maybe we want to have access to the previous state value:

```
const usePrevious = (value) => {
  const ref = useRef();

  useEffect(() => {
    // this will be changed after the value is returned
    ref.current = value;
  }, [value]);

  return ref.current;
};
```

And then trigger something conditionally in `useEffect:`

```
useEffect(() => {
  if (previuosValue.length > value.length) {
    console.log('Text was deleted');
  } else {
    console.log('Text was added');
  }
}, [previuosValue, value]);
```

Interactive example and full code
https://advanced-react.com/examples/09/04

And, of course, assign DOM elements to Ref. This is one of Ref's most important and most popular use cases.

Assigning DOM elements to Ref

We can do this as simply as creating a Ref with the `useRef` hook and then passing that Ref to a DOM element via the `ref` attribute:

```
const Component = () => {
  const ref = useRef(null);

  // assing ref to an input element
  return <input ref={ref} />;
};
```

After this `input` component is rendered, I will be able to see the actual `input` DOM element, exactly the same element that I would get from `getElementById`, in `ref.current` value:

```
const Component = () => {
  const ref = useRef(null);

  useEffect(() => {
    // this will be a reference to input DOM element!
    // exactly the same as if I did getElementById for it
    console.log(ref.current);
  });

  return <input ref={ref} />;
};
```

The important thing to remember here is that `ref` will be assigned only *after* the element is rendered by React and its associated DOM element is created. We need something to assign to that Ref, isn't it? That means that the `ref.current` value won't be available right away, and logic like this will just not work:

```
const Component = () => {
  const ref = useRef(null);

  // trying to access ref value before it was actually assigned
```

```
  // input will never be rendered here
  if (!ref.current) return null;

  return <input ref={ref} />;
};
```

We should only read and write `ref.current` either in the `useEffect` hook or in callbacks.

Finally, back to our initial idea of a fancy sign-up form. If I were implementing it as one giant component, I could do something like this:

```
const Form = () => {
  const [name, setName] = useState('');
  const ref = useRef(null);

  const onSubmitClick = () => {
    if (!name) {
      // focus the input field if someone tries to submit the empty
name
      ref.current.focus();
    } else {
      // submit the data here!
    }
  };

  return (
    <>
      ...
      <input
        onChange={(e) => setName(e.target.value)}
        ref={ref}
      />
      <button onClick={onSubmitClick}>
        Submit the form!
      </button>
    </>
  );
};
```

Store the values from inputs in the state, create refs for all inputs, and when the "submit" button is clicked, I would check whether the values are not empty, and if they are - focus the needed input.

Interactive example and full code
https://advanced-react.com/examples/09/05

Passing Ref from parent to child as a prop

Only in real life, I wouldn't do one giant component with everything, of course. More likely, I would want to extract that input into its own component: so that it can be reused across multiple forms, and can encapsulate and control its styles, maybe even have some additional features like having a label on the top or an icon on the right.

```
const InputField = ({ onChange, label }) => {
  return (
    <>
      {label}
      <br />
      <input
        type="text"
        onChange={(e) => onChange(e.target.value)}
      />
    </>
  );
};
```

But error handling and submitting functionality still going to be in the `Form`, not the input!

```
const Form = () => {
  const [name, setName] = useState('');

  const onSubmitClick = () => {
```

```
    if (!name) {
      // deal with empty name
    } else {
      // submit the data here!
    }
  };

  return (
    <>
      <InputField label="name" onChange={setName} />
      <button onClick={onSubmitClick}>
        Submit the form!
      </button>
    </>
  );
};
```

How can I tell the input to "focus itself" from the Form component? The "normal" way to control data and behavior in React is to pass props to components and listen to callbacks. I could try to pass the prop "focusItself" to `InputField` that I would switch from `false` to `true`, but that would only work once.

```
// don't do this! just to demonstate how it could work in theory
const InputField = ({ onChange, focusItself }) => {
  const inputRef = useRef(null);

  useEffect(() => {
    if (focusItself) {
      // focus input if the focusItself prop changes
      // will work only once, when false changes to true
      inputRef.current.focus();
    }
  }, [focusItself]);

  // the rest is the same here
};
```

I could try to add an "onBlur" callback and reset that `focusItself` prop to `false` when the input loses focus, or play around with random values instead of a boolean, or come up with some other creative solution.

Fortunately, there is another way. Instead of fiddling around with props, we can just create a Ref in one component (Form), pass it down to another component (InputField), and attach it to the underlying DOM element there. Ref is just a mutable object, after all.

Form would then create the Ref as normal:

```
const Form = () => {
  // create the Ref in Form component
  const inputRef = useRef(null);


  ...

}
```

And the InputField component will have a prop that accepts the Ref and will render an input field that expects a Ref as well. Only Ref there, instead of being created in InputField , will be coming from props:

```
const InputField = ({ inputRef }) => {
  // the rest of the code is the same

  // pass ref from prop to the internal input component
  return <input ref={inputRef} ... />
}
```

Ref is a *mutable* object and was designed that way. When we pass it to an element, React underneath just mutates it. And the object that is going to be mutated is declared in the Form component. So as soon as InputField is rendered, the Ref object will mutate, and our Form will have access to the input DOM element in inputRef.current :

```
const Form = () => {
  // create the Ref in Form component
  const inputRef = useRef(null);

  useEffect(() => {
```

```
    // the "input" element, that is rendered inside InputField, will
be here
    console.log(inputRef.current);
  }, []);

  return (
    <>
      {/* Pass Ref as prop to the input field component */}
      <InputField inputRef={inputRef} />
    </>
  );
};
```

Or in our submit callback, we can call `inputRef.current.focus()`, exactly the same code as before.

> **Interactive example and full code**
> https://advanced-react.com/examples/09/06

Passing Ref from parent to child with forwardRef

In case you're wondering why I named the prop `inputRef`, rather than just `ref`: it's actually not that simple. `ref` is not a real prop; it's kind of a "reserved" name. In the old days, when we were still writing class components, if we passed a Ref to a class component, this component's instance would be the `.current` value of that Ref.

But functional components don't have class instances. So instead, we just get a warning in the console: "Function components cannot be given refs. Attempts to access this ref will fail. Did you mean to use React.forwardRef()?"

```
const Form = () => {
  const inputRef = useRef(null);
```

```
  // if we just do this, we'll get a warning in console
  return <InputField ref={inputRef} />;
};
```

In order for this to work, we need to signal to React that this `ref` is actually intentional, and we want to do stuff with it. We can do it with the help of the `forwardRef` function: it accepts our component and *injects* the Ref from the `ref` attribute as a second argument of the component's function. Right after the props.

```
// normally, we'd have only props there
// but we wrapped the component's function with forwardRef
// which injects the second argument - ref
// if it's passed to this component by its consumer
const InputField = forwardRef((props, ref) => {
  // the rest of the code is the same

  return <input ref={ref} />;
});
```

We could even split the above code into two variables for better readability:

```
const InputFieldWithRef = (props, ref) => {
  // the rest is the same
};

// this one will be used by the form
export const InputField = forwardRef(InputFieldWithRef);
```

And now the `Form` can just pass the Ref to the `InputField` component as if it were a regular DOM element:

```
return <InputField ref={inputRef} />;
```

Whether you should use `forwardRef` or simply pass the Ref as a prop is just a matter of personal taste: the end result is the same.

Interactive example and full code
https://advanced-react.com/examples/09/07

Imperative API with useImperativeHandle

Okay, focusing the input from the `Form` component is sorted, kinda. But we are in no way done with our cool form. Remember, we wanted to shake the input in addition to focusing when an error happens? There is no such thing as `element.shake()` in the native JavaScript API, so access to the DOM element won't help here.

We could very easily implement it as a CSS animation though:

```
const InputField = () => {
  // store whether we should shake or not in state
  const [shouldShake, setShouldShake] = useState(false);

  // just add the classname when it's time to shake it - css will
handle it
  const className = shouldShake ? 'shake-animation' : '';

  // when animation is done - transition state back to false, so we
can start again if needed
  return (
    <input
      className={className}
      onAnimationEnd={() => setShouldShake(false)}
    />
  );
};
```

But how do we trigger it? Again, the same story as before with focus - I could come up with some creative solution using props, but it would look weird and significantly overcomplicate the `Form`. Especially considering that we're handling focus through ref, so we'd have two solutions for exactly

the same problem. If only I could do something like
`InputField.shake()` and `InputField.focus()` here!

Speaking of focus, why does my `Form` component still have to deal with the native DOM API to trigger it? Isn't it the responsibility and the whole point of the `InputField` to abstract away complexities like this? Why does the form even have to access the underlying DOM element - it's basically leaking internal implementation details. The `Form` component shouldn't care which DOM element we're using or whether we even use DOM elements or something else at all. Separation of concerns, you know.

Looks like it's time to implement a proper imperative API for our `InputField` component. React is declarative and expects us to write our code accordingly. But sometimes we just need a way to trigger something imperatively. Fortunately, React gives us an escape hatch for this: `useImperativeHandle` [9] hook.

This hook is slightly mind-boggling to understand. I had to read the docs twice, try it out a few times, and go through its implementation in the actual React code to really get what it's doing. But essentially, we just need two things: to decide how our imperative API will look like and a Ref to attach it to. For our input, it's simple: we need `.focus()` and `.shake()` functions as an API, and we already know all about refs.

```
// this is how our API could look like
const InputFieldAPI = {
  focus: () => {
    // do the focus here magic
  },
  shake: () => {
    // trigger shake here
  },
};
```

The `useImperativeHandle` hook simply attaches this object to the Ref object's "current" property, that's all. This is how it does it:

```
const InputField = () => {
```

```
useImperativeHandle(
  someRef,
  () => ({
    focus: () => {},
    shake: () => {},
  }),
  [],
);
};
```

The first argument is our Ref, which is either created in the component itself, passed from props, or through `forwardRef` . The second argument is a function that returns an object - this is the object that will be available as `inputRef.current` . The third argument is the array of dependencies, same as any other React hook.

For our component, let's pass the Ref explicitly as the `apiRef` prop. And the only thing that is left to do is to implement the actual API. For that, we'll need another Ref - this time internal to `InputField` , so that we can attach it to the `input` DOM element and trigger focus as usual:

```
// pass the Ref that we'll use as our imperative API as a prop
const InputField = ({ apiRef }) => {
  // create another Ref - internal to Input component
  const inputRef = useRef(null);

  // "merge" our API into the apiRef
  // the returned object will be available for use as apiRef.current
  useImperativeHandle(
    apiRef,
    () => ({
      focus: () => {
        // just trigger focus on internal Ref that is attached to the
DOM object
        inputRef.current.focus();
      },
      shake: () => {},
    }),
    [],
  );
```

```
  return <input ref={inputRef} />;
};
```

And for "shake," we'll just trigger the state update:

```
// pass the Ref that we'll use as our imperative API as a prop
const InputField = ({ apiRef }) => {
  // remember our state for shaking?
  const [shouldShake, setShouldShake] = useState(false);

  useImperativeHandle(apiRef, () => ({
    focus: () => {},
    shake: () => {
      // trigger state update here
      setShouldShake(true);
    },
  }), [])

  return ...
}
```

Voila! Our `Form` can just create a `ref`, pass it to `InputField`, and will be able to do simple `inputRef.current.focus()` and `inputRef.current.shake()`, without worrying about their internal implementation!

```
const Form = () => {
  const inputRef = useRef(null);
  const [name, setName] = useState('');

  const onSubmitClick = () => {
    if (!name) {
      // focus the input if the name is empty
      inputRef.current.focus();
      // and shake it off!
      inputRef.current.shake();
    } else {
      // submit the data here!
    }
```

```
  };

  return (
    <>
      <InputField
        label="name"
        onChange={setName}
        apiRef={inputRef}
      />
      <button onClick={onSubmitClick}>
        Submit the form!
      </button>
    </>
  );
};
```

Interactive example and full code
https://advanced-react.com/examples/09/08

Imperative API without useImperativeHandle

If the `useImperativeHandle` hook still makes your eye twitch - don't worry, mine twitches too! But we don't actually have to use it to implement the functionality we just implemented. We already know that a ref is just a mutable object, and we can assign anything to it. So all we need to do is just assign our API object to the `ref.current` of the needed Ref, something like this:

```
const InputField = ({ apiRef }) => {
  useEffect(() => {
    apiRef.current = {
      focus: () => {},
      shake: () => {},
    };
  }, [apiRef]);
```

```
};
```

This is almost exactly what `useImperativeHandle` does under the hood anyway. And it will work exactly like before.

Interactive example and full code
https://advanced-react.com/examples/09/09

Pretty cool trick, isn't it? Just remember: the imperative way to trigger something is more of an escape hatch in React. In 99% of cases, the normal props/callbacks data flow is more than enough.

Key takeaways

In the next chapter, we'll dive deeper into how to use Refs for storing functions rather than values, and what the consequences of that are. In the meantime, a few things to take away:

- A Ref is just a mutable object that can store any value. That value will be preserved between re-renders.
- A Ref's update doesn't trigger re-renders and is synchronous.
- We can assign a Ref to a DOM element via the `ref` attribute. After that element is rendered, we'll see that element in the `ref.current` property.
- We can pass Refs as regular props to any component.
- If we want to pass it as the actual ref prop, we need to wrap that component in `forwardRef`. Otherwise, it won't work on functional components. The second argument of that component will be the `ref` itself, which we then need to pass down to the desired DOM element.

```
// second argument, next to props, is ref that is injected by
"forwardRef"
const InputField = forwardRef((props, ref) => {
  return <input ref={ref} />;
```

```
});
```

- We can hide the implementation details of a component and expose its public API with the `useImperativeHandle` hook. We'll need to pass a Ref to that component, which will be mutated with the API properties:

```
const InputField = ({ apiRef }) => {
  useImperativeHandle(
    apiRef,
    () => ({
      focus: () => {},
      shake: () => {},
    }),
    [],
  );
};
```

- Or, we can always just mutate that Ref manually in the `useEffect` hook:

```
const InputField = ({ apiRef }) => {
  useEffect(() => {
    apiRef.current = {
      focus: () => {},
      shake: () => {},
    };
  }, [apiRef]);
};
```

Chapter 10. Closures in React

In the previous chapter, we learned everything about Refs: what they are, why we need them, when to use them, and when not to. However, when it comes to preserving something between re-renders, especially in Refs, there is one additional topic that we need to discuss: functions. More specifically, closures and how their existence affects our code.

Let's take a look at a few very interesting and quite typical bugs, how they appear, and in the process, learn:

- What closures are, how they appear, and why we need them.
- What a stale closure is, and why they occur.
- What the common scenarios in React are that cause stale closures, and how to fight them.

Warning: if you've never dealt with closures in React, this chapter might make your brain explode. Make sure to have enough chocolate with you to stimulate brain cells while you're reading this.

The problem

Imagine you're implementing a form with a few input fields. One of the fields is a very heavy component from some external library. You don't have access to its internals, so you can't fix its performance problems. But you really need it in your form, so you decide to wrap it in `React.memo`, to minimize its re-renders when the state in your form changes. Something like this:

```
const HeavyComponentMemo = React.memo(HeavyComponent);

const Form = () => {
  const [value, setValue] = useState();
```

```
  return (
    <>
      <input
        type="text"
        value={value}
        onChange={(e) => setValue(e.target.value)}
      />
      <HeavyComponentMemo />
    </>
  );
};
```

So far, so good. This Heavy component accepts just one string prop, let's say `title` , and an `onClick` callback. This one is triggered when you click a "done" button inside that component. And you want to submit your form data when this click happens. Also easy enough: just pass the `title` and `onClick` props to it.

```
const HeavyComponentMemo = React.memo(HeavyComponent);

const Form = () => {
  const [value, setValue] = useState();

  const onClick = () => {
    // submit our form data here
    console.log(value);
  };

  return (
    <>
      <input
        type="text"
        value={value}
        onChange={(e) => setValue(e.target.value)}
      />
      <HeavyComponentMemo
        title="Welcome to the form"
        onClick={onClick}
      />
    </>
```

```
  );
};
```

And now you'll face a dilemma. As we know from *Chapter 5. Memoization with useMemo, useCallback and React.memo*, every prop on a component wrapped in `React.memo` needs to be either a primitive value or persistent between re-renders. Otherwise, memoization won't work. So technically, we need to wrap our `onClick` in `useCallback`:

```
const onClick = useCallback(() => {
  // submit data here
}, []);
```

But also, we know that the `useCallback` hook should have all dependencies declared in its dependencies array. So if we want to submit our form data inside, we have to declare that data as a dependency:

```
const onClick = useCallback(() => {
  // submit data here
  console.log(value);

  // adding value to the dependency
}, [value]);
```

And here's the dilemma: even though our `onClick` is memoized, it still changes every time someone types in our input. So our performance optimization is useless.

Okay, fair enough, let's look for other solutions. `React.memo` has a thing called comparison function[10]. It allows us more granular control over props comparison in `React.memo`. Normally, React compares all "before" props with all "after" props by itself. If we provide this function, it will rely on its return result instead. If it returns `true`, then React will know that props are the same, and the component shouldn't be re-rendered. Sounds exactly what we need.

We only have one prop that we care about updating there, our `title`, so it's not going to be that complicated:

```
const HeavyComponentMemo = React.memo(
  HeavyComponent,
  (before, after) => {
    return before.title === after.title;
  },
);
```

The code for the entire form will then look something like this:

```
const HeavyComponentMemo = React.memo(
  HeavyComponent,
  (before, after) => {
    return before.title === after.title;
  },
);

const Form = () => {
  const [value, setValue] = useState();

  const onClick = () => {
    // submit our form data here
    console.log(value);
  };

  return (
    <>
      <input
        type="text"
        value={value}
        onChange={(e) => setValue(e.target.value)}
      />
      <HeavyComponentMemo
        title="Welcome to the form"
        onClick={onClick}
      />
    </>
  );
};
```

And it worked! We type something in the input, the heavy component doesn't re-render, and performance doesn't suffer.

Except for one tiny problem: it doesn't actually work. If you type something in the input and then press that button, the `value` that we log in `onClick` is `undefined`. But it can't be undefined, the input works as expected, and if I add `console.log` outside of `onClick` it logs it correctly. Just not inside `onClick`.

```
// those one logs it correctly
console.log(value);

const onClick = () => {
  // this is always undefined
  console.log(value);
};
```

Interactive example and full code
https://advanced-react.com/examples/10/01

What's going on?

This is known as the "stale closure" problem. And in order to fix it, we first need to dig a bit into probably the most feared topic in JavaScript: closures and how they work.

JavaScript, scope, and closures

Let's start with functions and variables. What happens when we declare a function in JavaScript, either via normal declaration or via arrow function?

```
function something() {
  //
}
const something = () => {};
```

By doing that, we created a *local scope:* an area in our code where variables declared inside won't be visible from the outside.

```
const something = () => {
  const value = 'text';
};

console.log(value); // not going to work, "value" is local to
"something" function
```

This happens every time we create a function. A function created inside another function will have its own local scope, invisible to the function outside.

```
const something = () => {
  const inside = () => {
    const value = 'text';
  };

  console.log(value); // not going to work, "value" is local to
"inside" function
};
```

In the opposite direction, however, it's an open road. The inner-most function will "see" all the variables declared outside.

```
const something = () => {
  const value = 'text';

  const inside = () => {
    // perfectly fine, value is available here
    console.log(value);
  };
};
```

This is achieved by creating what is known as "closure". The function inside "closes" over all the data from the outside. It's essentially a snapshot of all the "outside" data frozen in time stored separately in memory.

If instead of creating that `value` inside the `something` function, I pass it as an argument and return the `inside` function:

```
const something = (value) => {
  const inside = () => {
    // perfectly fine, value is available here
    console.log(value);
  };

  return inside;
};
```

We'll get this behavior:

```
const first = something('first');
const second = something('second');

first(); // logs "first"
second(); // logs "second"
```

We call our `something` function with the value "first" and assign the result to a variable. The result is a reference to a function declared inside. A closure is formed. From now on, as long as the `first` variable that holds that reference exists, the value "first" that we passed to it is frozen, and the `inside` function will have access to it.

The same story with the second call: we pass a different value, a closure is formed, and the function returned will forever have access to that variable.

This is true for any variable declared locally inside the `something` function:

```
const something = (value) => {
  const r = Math.random();

  const inside = () => {
    // ...
  };
};
```

```
    return inside;
};

const first = something('first');
const second = something('second');

first(); // logs random number
second(); // logs another random number
```

It's like taking a photograph of some dynamic scene: as soon as you press the button, the entire scene is "frozen" in the picture forever. The next press of the button will not change anything in the previously taken picture.

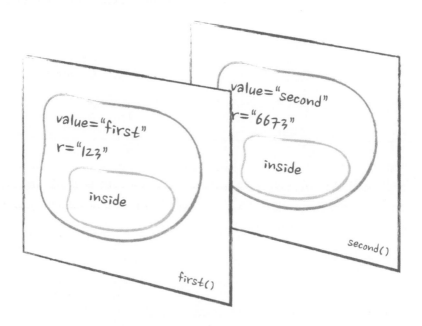

In React, we're creating closures all the time without even realizing it. Every single callback function declared inside a component is a closure:

```
const Component = () => {
  const onClick = () => {
    // closure!
  };
```

```
    return <button onClick={onClick} />;
  };
```

Everything in `useEffect` or `useCallback` hook is a closure:

```
  const Component = () => {
    const onClick = useCallback(() => {
      // closure!
    });

    useEffect(() => {
      // closure!
    });
  };
```

All of them will have access to state, props, and local variables declared in
the component:

```
  const Component = () => {
    const [state, setState] = useState();

    const onClick = useCallback(() => {
      // perfectly fine
      console.log(state);
    });

    useEffect(() => {
      // perfectly fine
      console.log(state);
    });
  };
```

Every single function inside a component is a closure since a component
itself is just a function.

The stale closure problem

But all of the above, although slightly unusual if you're coming from a language that doesn't have closures, is still relatively straightforward. You create a few functions a few times, and it becomes natural. It's even unnecessary to understand the concept of "closure" to write apps in React for years.

So what is the problem, then? Why are closures one of the most terrifying things in JavaScript and a source of pain for so many developers?

It's because closures live for as long as a reference to the function that caused them exists. And the reference to a function is just a value that can be assigned to anything. Let's twist our brains a bit. Here's our function from above, that returns a perfectly innocent closure:

```
const something = (value) => {
  const inside = () => {
    console.log(value);
  };

  return inside;
};
```

But the `inside` function is re-created there with every `something` call. What will happen if I decide to fight it and cache it? Something like this:

```
const cache = {};

const something = (value) => {
  if (!cache.current) {
    cache.current = () => {
      console.log(value);
    };
  }

  return cache.current;
};
```

On the surface, the code seems harmless. We just created an external variable named `cache` and assigned our inside function to the `cache.current` property. Now, instead of this function being re-created every time, we just return the already saved value.

However, if we try to call it a few times, we'll see a weird thing:

```
const first = something('first');
const second = something('second');
const third = something('third');

first(); // logs "first"
second(); // logs "first"
third(); // logs "first"
```

No matter how many times we call the `something` function with different arguments, the logged value is always the first one!

We just created what is known as the "stale closure". Every closure is frozen at the point when it's created. When we first called the `something` function, we created a closure that has "first" in the `value` variable. And then, we saved it in an object that sits outside of the `something` function.

When we call the `something` function the next time, instead of creating a new function with a new closure, we return the one that we created before. The one that was frozen with the "first" variable forever.

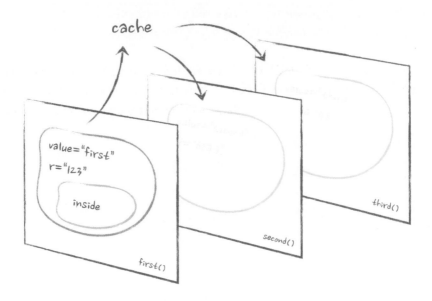

In order to fix this behavior, we'd want to re-create the function and its closure every time the value changes. Something like this:

```
const cache = {};
let prevValue;

const something = (value) => {
  // check whether the value has changed
  if (!cache.current || value !== prevValue) {
    cache.current = () => {
      console.log(value);
    };
  }

  // refresh it
  prevValue = value;
  return cache.current;
};
```

Save the value in a variable so that we can compare the next value with the previous one. And then refresh the cache.current closure if the variable has changed.

Now it will be logging variables correctly, and if we compare functions with the same value, that comparison will return `true` :

```
const first = something('first');
const anotherFirst = something('first');
const second = something('second');

first(); // logs "first"
second(); // logs "second"
console.log(first === anotherFirst); // will be true
```

Interactive example and full code
https://advanced-react.com/examples/10/02

Stale closures in React: useCallback

If you remember the *Memoization with useMemo, useCallback, and React.memo* chapter, the code above should look familiar. And indeed, we just implemented exactly what the `useCallback` hook does for us. Every time we use `useCallback` , we create a closure, and the function that we pass to it is cached:

```
// that inline function is cached exactly as in the section before
const onClick = useCallback(() => {}, []);
```

If we need access to state or props inside this function, we need to add them to the dependencies array:

```
const Component = () => {
  const [state, setState] = useState();

  const onClick = useCallback(() => {
    // access to state inside
    console.log(state);

    // need to add this to the dependencies array
```

```
  }, [state]);
};
```

This dependencies array is what makes React refresh that cached closure, exactly as we did when we compared `value !== prevValue`. If I forget about that array, our closure becomes stale:

```
const Component = () => {
  const [state, setState] = useState();

  const onClick = useCallback(() => {
    // state will always be the initial state value here
    // the closure is never refreshed
    console.log(state);

    // forgot about dependencies
  }, []);
};
```

And every time I trigger that callback, all that will be logged is `undefined`.

> **Interactive example and full code**
> https://advanced-react.com/examples/10/03

Stale closures in React: Refs

The second most common way to introduce the stale closure problem, after `useCallback` and `useMemo` hooks, is Refs.

What will happen if I try to use Ref for that `onClick` callback instead of `useCallback` hook? It's sometimes what the articles on the internet recommend doing to memoize props on components. On the surface, it does look simpler: just pass a function to `useRef` and access it through `ref.current`. No dependencies, no worries.

```
const Component = () => {
  const ref = useRef(() => {
    // click handler
  });

  // ref.current stores the function and is stable between re-renders
  return <HeavyComponent onClick={ref.current} />;
};
```

However. Every function inside our component will form a closure,
including the function that we pass to `useRef` . Our ref will be initialized
only once when it's created and never updated by itself. It's basically the
logic that we created at the beginning. Only instead of `value` , we pass the
function that we want to preserve. Something like this:

```
const ref = {};

const useRef = (callback) => {
  if (!ref.current) {
    ref.current = callback;
  }

  return ref.current;
};
```

So, in this case, the closure that was formed at the very beginning, when the
component was just mounted, will be preserved and never refreshed. When
we try to access the state or props inside that function stored in Ref, we'll
only get their initial values:

```
const Component = ({ someProp }) => {
  const [state, setState] = useState();

  const ref = useRef(() => {
    // both of them will be stale and will never change
    console.log(someProp);
    console.log(state);
  });
};
```

To fix this, we need to ensure that we update that ref value every time something that we try to access inside changes. Essentially, we need to implement what the dependencies array functionality does for the `useCallback` hook.

```
const Component = ({ someProp }) => {
  // initialize ref - creates closure!
  const ref = useRef(() => {
    // both of them will be stale and will never change
    console.log(someProp);
    console.log(state);
  });

  useEffect(() => {
    // update the closure when state or props change
    ref.current = () => {
      console.log(someProp);
      console.log(state);
    };
  }, [state, someProp]);
};
```

Interactive example and full code
https://advanced-react.com/examples/10/04

Stale closures in React: React.memo

And finally, we're back to the beginning of the chapter and the mystery that initiated all this. Let's take a look at the problematic code again:

```
const HeavyComponentMemo = React.memo(
  HeavyComponent,
  (before, after) => {
    return before.title === after.title;
  },
```

```
  );

const Form = () => {
  const [value, setValue] = useState();

  const onClick = () => {
    // submit our form data here
    console.log(value);
  };

  return (
    <>
      <input
        type="text"
        value={value}
        onChange={(e) => setValue(e.target.value)}
      />
      <HeavyComponentMemo
        title="Welcome to the form"
        onClick={onClick}
      />
    </>
  );
};
```

Every time we click on the button, we log "undefined". Our `value` inside `onClick` is never updated. Can you tell why now?

It's a stale closure again, of course. When we create `onClick`, the closure is first formed with the default state value, i.e., "undefined". We pass that closure to our memoized component, along with the `title` prop. Inside the comparison function, we compare only the `title`. It never changes, it's just a string. The comparison function always returns `true`, `HeavyComponent` is never updated, and as a result, it holds the reference to the very first `onClick` closure, with the frozen "undefined" value.

Now that we know the problem, how do we fix it? Easier said than done here...

Ideally, we should compare every prop in the comparison function, so we need to include `onClick` there:

```
(before, after) => {
  return (
    before.title === after.title &&
    before.onClick === after.onClick
  );
};
```

However, in this case, it would mean we're just reimplementing the React default behavior and doing exactly what `React.memo` without the comparison function does. So we can just ditch it and leave it only as `React.memo(HeavyComponent)`.

But doing that means that we need to wrap our `onClick` in `useCallback`. But it depends on the state, so it will change with every keystroke. We're back to square one: our heavy component will re-render on every state change, exactly what we tried to avoid.

We could play around with composition and try to extract and isolate either state or `HeavyComponent`. The techniques we explored in the first few chapters. But it won't be easy: input and `HeavyComponent` both depend on that state.

We can try many other things. But we don't have to do any heavy refactorings to escape that closures trap. There is one cool trick that can help us here.

Escaping the closure trap with Refs

This trick is absolutely mind-blowing: it's very simple, but it can forever change how you memoize functions in React. Or maybe not... In any case, it will be essential for the next chapter, so let's dive into it.

Let's get rid of the comparison function in our `React.memo` and `onClick` implementation for now. Just a pure component with state and memoized `HeavyComponent`:

```
const HeavyComponentMemo = React.memo(HeavyComponent);

const Form = () => {
  const [value, setValue] = useState();

  return (
    <>
        <input type="text" value={value} onChange={(e) =>
setValue(e.target.value)} />
        <HeavyComponentMemo title="Welcome to the form" onClick={...}
/>
    </>
  );
}
```

Now we need to add an `onClick` function that is stable between re-renders but also has access to the latest state without re-creating itself.

We're going to store it in Ref, so let's add it. Empty for now:

```
const Form = () => {
  const [value, setValue] = useState();

  // adding an empty ref
  const ref = useRef();
};
```

In order for the function to have access to the latest state, it needs to be re-created with every re-render. There is no getting away from it, it's the nature of closures, nothing to do with React. We're supposed to modify Refs inside `useEffect`, not directly in render, so let's do that.

```
const Form = () => {
  const [value, setValue] = useState();

  // adding an empty ref
  const ref = useRef();
```

```
useEffect(() => {
  // our callback that we want to trigger
  // with state
  ref.current = () => {
    console.log(value);
  };

  // no dependencies array!
});
};
```

useEffect without the dependency array will be triggered on every re-render. Which is exactly what we want. So now in our ref.current we have a closure that is recreated with every re-render, so the state that is logged there is always the latest.

But we can't just pass that ref.current to the memoized component. That value will differ with every re-render, so memoization just won't work.

```
const Form = () => {
  const ref = useRef();

  useEffect(() => {
    ref.current = () => {
      console.log(value);
    };
  });

  return (
    <>
      {/* Can't do that, will break memoization */}
      <HeavyComponentMemo onClick={ref.current} />
    </>
  );
};
```

So instead, let's create a small empty function wrapped in useCallback with no dependencies for that.

```
const Form = () => {
  const ref = useRef();

  useEffect(() => {
    ref.current = () => {
      console.log(value);
    };
  });

  const onClick = useCallback(() => {
    // empty dependency! will never change
  }, []);

  return (
    <>
      {/* Now memoization will work, onClick never changes */}
      <HeavyComponentMemo onClick={onClick} />
    </>
  );
};
```

Now, memoization works perfectly - the `onClick` never changes. One problem, though: it does nothing.

And here's the magic trick: all we need to make it work is to call `ref.current` inside that memoized callback:

```
useEffect(() => {
  ref.current = () => {
    console.log(value);
  };
});

const onClick = useCallback(() => {
  // call the ref here
  ref.current();

  // still empty dependencies array!
}, []);
```

Notice how `ref` is not in the dependencies of the `useCallback` ? It doesn't need to be. `ref` by itself never changes. It's just a reference to a mutable object that the `useRef` hook returns.

But when a closure freezes everything around it, it doesn't make objects immutable or frozen. Objects are stored in a different part of the memory, and multiple variables can contain references to exactly the same object.

```
const a = { value: 'one' };
// b is a different variable that references the same object
const b = a;
```

If I mutate the object through one of the references and then access it through another, the changes will be there:

```
a.value = 'two';

console.log(b.value); // will be "two"
```

In our case, even that doesn't happen: we have exactly the same reference inside `useCallback` and inside `useEffect` . So when we mutate the `current` property of the `ref` object inside `useEffect` , we can access that exact property inside our `useCallback` . This property happens to be a closure that captured the latest state data.

The full code will look like this:

```
const Form = () => {
  const [value, setValue] = useState();
  const ref = useRef();

  useEffect(() => {
    ref.current = () => {
      // will be latest
      console.log(value);
    };
  });

  const onClick = useCallback(() => {
```

```
    // will be latest
    ref.current?.();
  }, []);

  return (
    <>
      <input
        type="text"
        value={value}
        onChange={(e) => setValue(e.target.value)}
      />
      <HeavyComponentMemo
        title="Welcome closures"
        onClick={onClick}
      />
    </>
  );
};
```

Now, we have the best of both worlds: the heavy component is properly memoized and doesn't re-render with every state change. And the `onClick` callback on it has access to the latest data in the component without ruining memoization. We can safely send everything we need to the backend now!

Interactive example and full code
https://advanced-react.com/examples/10/05

Key takeaways

Hopefully, all of this made sense, and closures are now easy-peasy for you. In the next chapter, we'll take a look at another very useful use case for escaping the closures trap: debouncing and throttling callbacks. But before that, let's remember:

- Closures are formed every time a function is created inside another function.

- Since React components are just functions, every function created inside forms a closure, including such hooks as `useCallback` and `useRef`.
- When a function that forms a closure is called, all the data around it is "frozen", like a snapshot.
- To update that data, we need to re-create the "closed" function. This is what dependencies of hooks like `useCallback` allow us to do.
- If we miss a dependency, or don't refresh the closed function assigned to `ref.current`, the closure becomes "stale".
- We can escape the "stale closure" trap in React by taking advantage of the fact that Ref is a mutable object. We can mutate `ref.current` outside of the stale closure, and then access it inside. Will be the latest data.

Chapter 11. Implementing advanced debouncing and throttling with Refs

In the previous chapters, we covered in detail what Ref is, how to use it, and how not to use it. There is, however, one very important and quite common use case for Refs that we haven't covered yet. It's storing various timers and timeout ids when dealing with functions like `setInterval` or `debounce`. It's a very common scenario for various form elements. We usually would want to debounce/throttle inputs' `onChange` callbacks, for example, so that the form is not re-rendered with every keystroke.

And implementing debouncing/throttling in React properly is quite challenging, actually. You can't just wrap an `onChange` callback in `debounce` imported from the `lodash` library and expect everything to work. So in this chapter, let's try to implement a good `useDebounce` hook and see what challenges and common caveats await us on the way. I'm going to use `debounce` and `throttle` functions from the Lodash library[11] and focus on React-specific things here.

While doing so, we'll learn:

- What debouncing and throttling are, and what the difference between them is (a very quick knowledge refresh).
- Why we can't just use `debounce` directly on our event handlers.
- How to use `useMemo` or `useCallback` for that, and what the downsides of those are.
- How to use Refs for debouncing, and what the difference between Refs and using `useMemo` and `useCallback` is.
- How to use the closure trap escape trick for implementing debouncing.

What are debouncing and throttling?

Let's briefly refresh what "debounce" and "throttle" are, just in case you haven't had a chance to use them yet. "Debouncing" and "Throttling"[12] are techniques that allow us to skip function execution if that function is called too many times over a certain time period.

Imagine, for example, that we're implementing a simple asynchronous search functionality: an input field, where a user can type something, and while they are doing so, the text is sent to the backend, which in turn returns relevant search results. We can surely implement it "naively", with just an input field and `onChange` callback:

```
const Input = () => {
  const onChange = (e) => {
    // send data from input field to the backend here
    // will be triggered on every keystroke
  };
  return <input onChange={onChange} />;
};
```

But a skilled typist can type at the speed of 70 words per minute, which is roughly 6 keypresses per second. In this implementation, it will result in 6 `onChange` events, i.e., 6 requests to the server per second! Not every backend can handle that. Nor does it need to.

Instead of sending that request on every keypress, we can wait a little bit until the user stops typing, and then send the entire value in one go. This is what debouncing does. If I apply debounce to my `onChange` function, it will detect every attempt I make to call it, and if the waiting interval hasn't passed yet, it will drop the previous call and restart the "waiting" clock.

```
const Input = () => {
  const onChange = (e) => {
    // send data from input field to the backend here
    // will be triggered 500 ms after the user stopped typing
  };
```

```
  const debouncedOnChange = debounce(onChange, 500);

  return <input onChange={debouncedOnChange} />;
};
```

Before, if I was typing "React" in the search field, the requests to the backend would be on every keypress instantaneously, with the values "R", "Re", "Rea", "Reac", "React". Now, after I debounced it, it will wait 500 ms after I stopped typing "React" and then send only one request with the value "React".

Underneath, debounce is just a function that accepts a function, returns another function, and has a tracker inside that detects whether the passed function was called sooner than the provided interval. If sooner - then skip the execution and re-start the clock. If the interval has passed, call the passed function. Essentially, it's something like this:

```
const debounce = (callback, wait) => {
  // initialize the timer
  let timer;

  // lots of code here involving the actual implementation of timer
  // to track the time passed since the last callback call

  const debouncedFunc = () => {
    // checking whether the waiting time has passed
    if (shouldCallCallback(Date.now())) {
      callback();
    } else {
      // if time hasn't passed yet, restart the timer
      timer = startTimer(callback);
    }
  };

  return debouncedFunc;
};
```

The actual implementation is, of course, a bit more complicated. You can check out the lodash debounce code[13] to get a sense of it.

`Throttle` is very similar, and the idea of keeping the internal tracker and a function that returns a function is the same. The difference is that `throttle` guarantees to call the callback function regularly, every `wait` interval, whereas `debounce` will constantly reset the timer and wait until the end.

The difference will be obvious if we use not an async search example, but an editing field with auto-save functionality: if a user types something in the field, we want to send requests to the backend to save whatever they type "on the fly", without them pressing the "save" button explicitly. If a user is writing a poem in a field like that really, really fast, the "debounced" `onChange` callback will be triggered only once. And if something breaks while typing, the entire poem will be lost. The "throttled" callback will be triggered periodically, the poem will be regularly saved, and if a disaster occurs, only the last milliseconds of the poem will be lost. Much safer approach.

> **Interactive example and full code**
> https://advanced-react.com/examples/11/01

Debounced callback in React: dealing with re-renders

Now that it's a bit more clear what debounce and throttle are, why we need them, and how they are implemented, it's time to dig deep into how they should be used in React. And I hope you don't think now "Oh c'mon, how hard can it be, it's just a function", do you? What our life would be without a surprise here and there.

First of all, let's take a closer look at the `Input` implementation that has a debounced `onChange` callback (from now forward, I'll only use `debounce` in all examples; every concept described will also be relevant for throttle).

```
const Input = () => {
```

```
  const onChange = (e) => {
    // send data from input to the backend here
  };

  const debouncedOnChange = debounce(onChange, 500);

  return <input onChange={debouncedOnChange} />;
};
```

While the example works perfectly and seems like regular React code with no caveats, it unfortunately has nothing to do with real life. In real life, more likely than not, you'd want to do something with the value from the input other than sending it to the backend. Maybe this input will be part of a large form. Or you'd want to introduce a "clear" button there. Or maybe the `input` tag is actually a component from some external library that mandatory asks for the `value` field.

What I'm trying to say here is that at some point, you'd want to save that value into the state, either in the `Input` component itself or pass it to parent/external state management to manage it instead. Let's do it in the `Input` component for simplicity.

```
const Input = () => {
  // adding state for the value
  const [value, setValue] = useState();

  const onChange = (e) => {};
  const debouncedOnChange = debounce(onChange, 500);

  // turning input into controlled component by passing value from
  state there
  return (
    <input onChange={debouncedOnChange} value={value} />
  );
};
```

I added a state `value` via the `useState` hook and passed that value to the `input` field. One thing left to do is for the `input` to update that state on typing. Otherwise, the input won't work. Normally, without debounce, it would be done in the `onChange` callback:

```
const Input = () => {
  const [value, setValue] = useState();

  const onChange = (e) => {
    // set state value from onChange event
    setValue(e.target.value);
  };

  return <input onChange={onChange} value={value} />;
};
```

I can't do that in a debounced `onChange` : its call is by definition delayed, so the `value` in the state won't be updated on time, and the `input` just won't work.

```
const Input = () => {
  const [value, setValue] = useState();

  const onChange = (e) => {
    // just won't work, this callback is debounced
    setValue(e.target.value);
  };
  const debouncedOnChange = debounce(onChange, 500);

  return (
    <input onChange={debouncedOnChange} value={value} />
  );
};
```

I have to call `setValue` immediately when `input` calls its own `onChange` . This means I can't debounce our `onChange` function anymore in its entirety and can only debounce the part that I actually need to slow down: sending requests to the backend.

Probably something like this, right?

```
const Input = () => {
  const [value, setValue] = useState();

  const sendRequest = (value) => {
    // send value to the backend
  };

  // now send request is debounced
  const debouncedSendRequest = debounce(sendRequest, 500);

  // onChange is not debounced anymore, it just calls debounced
function
  const onChange = (e) => {
    const value = e.target.value;

    // state is updated on every value change, so input will work
    setValue(value);

    // call debounced request here
    debouncedSendRequest(value);
  };

  return <input onChange={onChange} value={value} />;
};
```

Seems logical. Only... it doesn't work either! Now the request is not debounced at all, just delayed a bit. If I type "React" in this field, I will still send all "R", "Re", "Rea", "Reac", "React" requests instead of just one "React," as a properly debounced function should, only delayed by half a second.

Interactive example and full code
https://advanced-react.com/examples/11/02

The answer is, of course, re-renders (it usually is in React). As we know from the first chapter, a state change will cause a component to re-render itself. With the introduction of state to manage value, we now re-render the entire `Input` component on every keystroke. As a result, on every keystroke, we now call the actual `debounce` function, not just the debounced callback. And, as we just discussed, the `debounce` function when called:

- creates a new timer
- creates and returns a function inside of which the passed callback will be called when the timer is done

So when on every re-render we're calling `debounce(sendRequest, 500)`, we're re-creating everything: new call, new timer, new return function with callback in arguments. But the old function is never cleaned up, so it just sits there in memory and waits for its timer to pass. When its timer is done, it fires the callback function and then just dies and eventually gets cleaned up by the garbage collector.

What we ended up with is just a simple `delay` function, rather than a proper `debounce`. The fix for it should seem obvious now: we should call `debounce(sendRequest, 500)` only once, to preserve the inside timer and the returned function.

The easiest way to do it would be just to move it outside of the `Input` component:

```
const sendRequest = (value) => {
  // send value to the backend
};
const debouncedSendRequest = debounce(sendRequest, 500);

const Input = () => {
  const [value, setValue] = useState();

  const onChange = (e) => {
    const value = e.target.value;
    setValue(value);

    // debouncedSendRequest is created once, so state caused re-
renders won't affect it anymore
    debouncedSendRequest(value);
  };
```

```
      return <input onChange={onChange} value={value} />;
  };
```

This won't work, however, if those functions have dependencies on something that is happening within the component's lifecycle, i.e. state or props. No problem though, we can use memoization hooks to achieve exactly the same result:

```
const Input = () => {
  const [value, setValue] = useState('initial');

  // memoize the callback with useCallback
  // we need it since it's a dependency in useMemo below
  const sendRequest = useCallback((value: string) => {
    console.log('Changed value:', value);
  }, []);

  // memoize the debounce call with useMemo
  const debouncedSendRequest = useMemo(() => {
    return debounce(sendRequest, 1000);
  }, [sendRequest]);

  const onChange = (e) => {
    const value = e.target.value;
    setValue(value);
    debouncedSendRequest(value);
  };

  return <input onChange={onChange} value={value} />;
};
```

Interactive example and full code
https://advanced-react.com/examples/11/03

Now everything is working as expected! The `Input` component has state, the backend call in `onChange` is debounced, and the debounce actually behaves properly.

Until it doesn't...

Debounced callback in React: dealing with state inside

Now to the final piece of this bouncing puzzle. Let's take a look at this code:

```
const sendRequest = useCallback((value: string) => {
  console.log('Changed value:', value);
}, []);
```

A normal memoized function that accepts `value` as an argument and then does something with it. The value is coming directly from `input` through the debounced function. We pass it when we call the debounced function within our `onChange` callback:

```
const onChange = (e) => {
  const value = e.target.value;
  setValue(value);

  // value is coming from input change event directly
  debouncedSendRequest(value);
};
```

But we have this value in state as well. Can't I just use it from there? Maybe I have a chain of those callbacks, and it's really hard to pass this value over and over through it. Maybe I want to have access to another state variable. It wouldn't make sense to pass it through a callback like this. Or maybe I just hate callbacks and arguments and want to use state just because. Should be simple enough, isn't it?

And of course, yet again, nothing is as simple as it seems. If I just get rid of the argument and use the `value` from the state, I would have to add it to the dependencies of the `useCallback` hook:

```
const Input = () => {
```

```
const [value, setValue] = useState('initial');

const sendRequest = useCallback(() => {
  // value is now coming from state
  console.log('Changed value:', value);

  // adding it to dependencies
}, [value]);
};
```

Because of that, the `sendRequest` function will change with every value change. This is how memoization works. The value is the same throughout the re-renders until the dependency changes. This means our memoized debounce call will now change constantly as well: it has `sendRequest` as a dependency, which now changes with every state update.

```
// this will now change on every state update
// because sendRequest has dependency on state
const debouncedSendRequest = useMemo(() => {
  return debounce(sendRequest, 1000);
}, [sendRequest]);
```

We've returned to where we were when we first introduced state to the `Input` component: debounce has turned into just a delay.

> **Interactive example and full code**
> https://advanced-react.com/examples/11/04

Is there anything that can be done here? Of course! It's a perfect usecase for Refs. If you search for articles about debouncing and React, half of them will mention `useRef` as a way to avoid re-creating the debounced function on every re-render.

Usually, the pattern goes like this:

```
const Input = () => {
  // creating ref and initializing it with the debounced backend call
```

```
  const ref = useRef(
    debounce(() => {
      // this is our old "debouncedSendRequest" function
    }, 500),
  );

  const onChange = (e) => {
    const value = e.target.value;

    // calling the debounced function
    ref.current();
  };
};
```

This might be actually a good alternative to the previous solution based on `useMemo` and `useCallback`. I don't know about you, but those chains of hooks give me a headache sometimes. The ref-based solution seems much simpler.

Unfortunately, it will only work for the previous use-case: when we didn't have state inside the callback. Remember the previous chapter and the closures problem? A Ref's initial value is cached and never updated. It's "frozen" at the time when the component is mounted and `ref` is initialized.

As we already know, when using functions in Refs, we need to update them in `useEffect`. Otherwise, the closure becomes stale.

```
const Input = () => {
  const [value, setValue] = useState();

  // creating ref and initializing it with the debounced backend call
  const ref = useRef(
    debounce(() => {
      // send request to the backend here
    }, 500),
  );

  useEffect(() => {
    // updating ref when state changes
```

```
    ref.current = debounce(() => {
      // send request to the backend here
    }, 500);
  }, [value]);

  const onChange = (e) => {
    const value = e.target.value;

    // calling the debounced function
    ref.current();
  };
};
```

But unfortunately, this is no different than the `useCallback` with
dependencies solution: the debounced function is re-created every time, the
timer inside is re-created every time, and debounce is nothing more than a
renamed `delay` .

Interactive example and full code
https://advanced-react.com/examples/11/05

One way to solve it would be to use a cleanup function in `useEffect`
(we'll talk more about those in *Chapter 15. Data fetching and race
conditions*), and reset the debounced callback before re-assigning it.
Something like this:

```
useEffect(() => {
  // updating ref when state changes
  ref.current = debounce(() => {}, 500);

  // cancel the debounce callback before
  return () => ref.current.cancel();
}, [value]);
```

In this case, with every update we're getting rid of the "old" debounced
closure, and starting a new one. Good solution for debouncing. But it won't
work for throttling unfortunately. If I keep canceling it, it will never have a

chance to be fired after the interval it's supposed to be fired, as throttle should. I want something more universal.

Another good use case for the solution to escape the closures trap, which we looked into in detail in the previous chapter! All we need to do is assign our `sendRequest` to Ref, update that Ref in `useEffect` to get access to the latest closure, and then trigger `ref.current` *inside* of our closure. Remember: refs are mutable, and closures don't perform deep cloning. Only the reference to that mutable object is "frozen", we're still free to mutate the object it points to every time.

Thinking in closures breaks my brain, but it actually works, and it's easier to follow that train of thought in code:

```
const Input = () => {
  const [value, setValue] = useState();

  const sendRequest = () => {
    // send request to the backend here
    // value is coming from state
    console.log(value);
  };

  // creating ref and initializing it with the sendRequest function
  const ref = useRef(sendRequest);

  useEffect(() => {
    // updating ref when state changes
    // now, ref.current will have the latest sendRequest with access
    to the latest state
    ref.current = sendRequest;
  }, [value]);

  // creating debounced callback only once - on mount
  const debouncedCallback = useMemo(() => {
    // func will be created only once - on mount
    const func = () => {
      // ref is mutable! ref.current is a reference to the latest
      sendRequest
      ref.current?.();
```

```
  };
  // debounce the func that was created once, but has access to the
latest sendRequest
    return debounce(func, 1000);
    // no dependencies! never gets updated
  }, []);

  const onChange = (e) => {
    const value = e.target.value;

    // calling the debounced function
    debouncedCallback();
  };
};
```

Now, all we need to do is extract that mind-numbing madness of closures into one tiny hook, put it in a separate file, and pretend not to notice it.

```
const useDebounce = (callback) => {
  const ref = useRef();

  useEffect(() => {
    ref.current = callback;
  }, [callback]);

  const debouncedCallback = useMemo(() => {
    const func = () => {
      ref.current?.();
    };

    return debounce(func, 1000);
  }, []);

  return debouncedCallback;
};
```

Then our production code can just use it without the eye-bleeding chain of useMemo and useCallback, without worrying about dependencies, and with access to the latest state and props inside!

```
const Input = () => {
  const [value, setValue] = useState();

  const debouncedRequest = useDebounce(() => {
    // send request to the backend
    // access to the latest state here
    console.log(value);
  });

  const onChange = (e) => {
    const value = e.target.value;
    setValue(value);

    debouncedRequest();
  };

  return <input onChange={onChange} value={value} />;
};
```

> **Interactive example and full code**
> https://advanced-react.com/examples/11/06

The power of closures and mutability in JavaScript is endless!

Key takeaways

That was fun, wasn't it? JavaScript's closures have to be the most loved
feature on the internet. In the next chapter, we'll try to recover from dealing
with them and play around with some UI improvements instead. More
specifically, we're going to learn how to get rid of the "flickering" effect for
positioned elements. But before that, let's quickly recap this chapter:

- We use debounce and throttle when we want to skip some function's
  executions that were fired too often.
- In order for those functions to work properly, they should be called
  only once in a component's life, usually when it's mounted.

- If we call them in the component's render function directly, the timer inside will be re-created with every re-render, and the functions will not work as expected.
- To fix this, we can memoize those with `useMemo` or through the usage of Refs.
- If we simply memoize them or use Refs "naively", we won't have access to the component's latest data, like state or props. This is happening because a closure is created when we initialize Ref, which freezes values at the time it's created.
- To escape the closure trap, we can leverage the mutable nature of the Ref object and gain access to the latest data by constantly updating the "closed" function in `ref.current` within `useEffect`.

Chapter 12. Escaping Flickering UI with useLayoutEffect

Let's talk a bit more about DOM access in React. In previous chapters, we covered how to do it with Ref and learned everything about Ref as a bonus. There is, however, another very important, although quite rare, topic when it comes to dealing with the DOM: changing elements based on real DOM measurements like the size or position of an element.

So, what is the problem with it, exactly, and why are "normal" tactics not good enough? Let's do some coding and figure it out. In the process, we'll learn:

- Everything we need to know about `useLayoutEffect`.
- When and why we'd want to use it instead of `useEffect`.
- How browsers render our React code.
- What painting is and why all of this matters.
- How SSR plays a role here.

What is the problem with useEffect?

It's coding time! Let's do something fancy: a responsive navigation component. It can render a row of links and can adjust the number of those links based on the container size.

And if some links don't fit, show a "more" button that will open them in a dropdown menu if clicked.

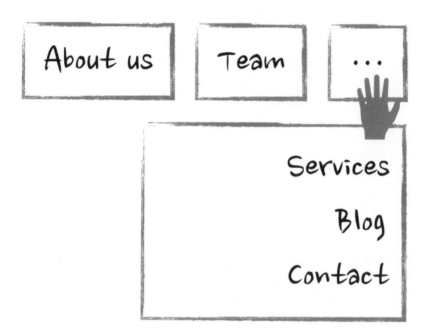

Now, the component itself. It's going to be just a component that accepts an array of data and renders proper links:

```
const Component = ({ items }) => {
  return (
    <div className="navigation">
      {items.map((item) => (
        <a href={item.href}>{item.name}</a>
      ))}
    </div>
  );
};
```

Now, how do we make it responsive? The problem here is that we need to calculate how many items will fit in the available space. In order to do that, we need to know the width of the container where they are rendered and the dimensions of every item. We can't assume anything in advance here, by counting letters for example: how text renders in the browser will depend heavily on the font used, language, browser, and probably even the phases of the moon.

The only way to get the actual sizes is to make the browser render the items and then extract the sizes via a native JavaScript API, like `getBoundingClientRect`.

We'd have to do it in a few steps. First, get access to the elements. We can create a Ref and assign it to the div that wraps those items:

```
const Component = ({ items }) => {
  const ref = useRef(null);

  return (
    <div className="navigation" ref={ref}>
      ...
    </div>
  );
};
```

Second, in `useEffect`, grab the div element and get its size.

```
const Component = ({ items }) => {

  useEffect(() => {
    const div = ref.current;
    const { width } = div.getBoundingClientRect();
  }, [ref]);

  return ...
}
```

Third, iterate over the div's children and extract their widths into an array.

```
const Component = ({ items }) => {

  useEffect(() => {
    // same code as before
```

```
    // convert div's children into an array
    const children = [...div.childNodes];
    // all the widths
    const childrenWidths = children.map(child =>
  child.getBoundingClientRect().width)
  }, [ref]);

  return ...
}
```

Now, all we need to do is iterate over that array, sum the widths of the children, compare those sums with the parent div, and find the last visible item as a result.

But wait, there is one thing we forgot: the "more" button. We need to take its width into account as well. Otherwise, we might find ourselves in a situation where a few items fit, but the "more" button doesn't.

Again, we can only get its width if we render it in the browser. So we have to add the button explicitly during the initial render:

```
const Component = ({ items }) => {
  return (
    <div className="navigation">
      {items.map((item) => (
        <a href={item.href}>{item.name}</a>
      ))}
      {/* add the "more" button after the links explicitly */}
      <button id="more">...</button>
    </div>
```

```
  );
};
```

If we abstract all the logic of calculating widths into a function, we'll end up with something like this in our `useEffect`:

```
useEffect(() => {
  const itemIndex = getLastVisibleItem(ref.current);
}, [ref]);
```

Where `getLastVisibleItem` function does all the math and returns us a single number - the index of the last link that can fit into the available space. I'm not going to dive into the logic itself. There are a million ways to do it, it will be available in the final code example a little further on.

The important thing here is that we've got that number. What should we do next from the React perspective? If we leave it as is, all links and the "more" button will be visible. And there's only one solution here - we need to trigger an update of the component and make it remove all those items that are not supposed to be there.

And there is pretty much the only way to do it: we need to save that number in the state when we get it:

```
const Component = ({ items }) => {
  // set the initial value to -1, to indicate that we haven't run the
calculations yet
  const [lastVisibleMenuItem, setLastVisibleMenuItem] =
    useState(-1);

  useEffect(() => {
    const itemIndex = getLastVisibleItem(ref.current);
    // update state with the actual number
    setLastVisibleMenuItem(itemIndex);
  }, [ref]);
};
```

And then, when rendering the menu, take that into account:

```
const Component = ({ items }) => {

  // render everything if it's the first pass and the value is still
  the default
  if (lastVisibleMenuItem === -1) {
    // render all of them here, same as before
    return ...
  }

  // show "more" button if the last visible item is not the last one
  in the array
  const isMoreVisible = lastVisibleMenuItem < items.length - 1;

  // filter out those items which index is more than the last visible
  const filteredItems = items.filter((item, index) => index <=
  lastVisibleMenuItem);

  return (
    <div className="navigation">
      {/*render only visible items*/}
      {filteredItems.map(item => <a href={item.href}>{item.name}</a>)}
      {/*render "more" conditionally*/}
      {isMoreVisible && <button id="more">...</button>}
    </div>
  )
}
```

That's about it! Now, after the state is updated with the actual number, it will trigger a re-render of the navigation, and React will re-render items and remove those that aren't visible. For a "proper" responsive experience, we would also need to listen for the resize event and re-calculate the number, but I'll leave that for you to implement.

You can find the full working example in the link below. With resize. Only don't get too excited just yet: there is one major flaw in the user experience here.

Interactive example and full code
https://advanced-react.com/examples/12/01

Try to refresh it a few times, especially with the slowed-down CPU. Unfortunately, there is a noticeable flash of content there. You should be able to clearly see that initial render - when all the items in the menu and the "more" button are visible. We definitely need to fix this before it goes into production.

Fixing it with useLayoutEffect

The reason for that flash should be pretty obvious: we render those items and make them visible before removing unnecessary items. And we have to render them first, otherwise, the fancy responsiveness won't work. So one possible fix would be to still render that first pass, but invisibly: with opacity set to 0, or in some div somewhere outside the visible area. And only after we extract the dimensions and the magic number, make them visible. This is how we used to handle cases like this in the past.

In React version from ~16.8 (the one with the hooks), however, all we need to do is replace our `useEffect` hook with `useLayoutEffect`.

```
const Component = ({ items }) => {
  // everything is exactly the same, only the hook name is different
  useLayoutEffect(() => {
    // the code is still the same
  }, [ref]);
};
```

This is pure magic, no more initial flashing.

Interactive example and full code
https://advanced-react.com/examples/12/02

Is it safe to do, though? Why don't we just use it everywhere instead of `useEffect`? The docs explicitly say that `useLayoutEffect` can hurt performance[14] and should be avoided. Why is that? It also says that it is fired "before the browser repaints the screen," which implies that `useEffect` is fired after. But what exactly does this mean in a practical sense? Do I need to think about low-level concepts like browser painting when writing simple dropdowns now?

To answer those questions, we need to step aside from React for a moment and talk about browsers and good old JavaScript instead.

Why the fix works: rendering, painting, and browsers

The first thing we need here is "browser rendering." In the React world, it is also known as "painting" just to differentiate it from React's rendering - those are very different! The idea here is relatively straightforward. Browsers don't continuously update everything that needs to be shown on the screen in real-time. It's not like drawing on a whiteboard, where you draw lines, erase lines, write some text, or sketch an owl.

Instead, it's more like showing slides to people: you show one slide, wait for them to comprehend the genius idea on it, then transition to the next slide, and so on.

Only they do it really, really fast. Normally, modern browsers try to maintain a 60 FPS rate, 60 frames per second. One slide changes to the next one ~every 13 milliseconds. This is what we refer to as "painting" in React.

The information that updates these slides is split into "tasks." Tasks are put in a queue. The browser grabs a task from the queue and executes it. If it has more time, it executes the next task, and so on, until no more time is left in that ~13ms gap, and then it refreshes the screen. And continues, non-stop, working tirelessly so that we can do such important things as doom-scrolling on Twitter without even noticing the effort it took.

What is a "task"? When it comes to normal JavaScript, it's everything that we put in the `script` tag and execute synchronously. Consider this code:

```
const app = document.getElementById('app');
```

```
const child = document.createElement('div');
child.innerHTML = '<h1>Heyo!</h1>';
app.appendChild(child);

child.style = 'border: 10px solid red';
child.style = 'border: 20px solid green';
child.style = 'border: 30px solid black';
```

I grab an element by its `id`, store it in the `app` variable, create a `div`, update its HTML, append that div to the app, and change the div's border three times. The *entire* thing will be considered as just one task for the browser. So it will execute every single line, and only then draw the final result: the div with the black border.

You won't be able to see this red-green-black transition on the screen.

What will happen if a "task" takes longer than 13ms? Well, that's unfortunate. The browser can't stop it or split it. It will continue with it until it's done, and then paint the final result. If I add 1-second synchronous delays between those border updates:

```
const waitSync = (ms) => {
  let start = Date.now(),
    now = start;
  while (now - start < ms) {
    now = Date.now();
  }
};

child.style = 'border: 10px solid red';
waitSync(1000);
child.style = 'border: 20px solid green';
waitSync(1000);
child.style = 'border: 30px solid black';
waitSync(1000);
```

we still won't be able to see the "in-between" result. We'll just stare at the blank screen until the browser sorts it out and enjoy the final black border in the end. This is what we refer to as "blocking render" or "blocking painting" code.

Interactive example and full code
https://advanced-react.com/examples/12/03

Now, although React is just JavaScript, it's not executed as one single task, of course. The internet would be unbearable if it was. We all would be forced to play outside and interact in person, and who wants that, really? The way to "break" a giant task like rendering an entire app into smaller ones is by using various "asynchronous" methods: callbacks, event handlers, promises, and so on.

If I simply wrap those style adjustments in `setTimeout`, even with 0 delay:

```
setTimeout(() => {
  child.style = 'border: 10px solid red';
  wait(1000);
  setTimeout(() => {
    child.style = 'border: 20px solid green';
    wait(1000);
    setTimeout(() => {
      child.style = 'border: 30px solid black';
      wait(1000);
    }, 0);
  }, 0);
}, 0);
```

Then every one of those timeouts will be considered a new "task." So the browser will be able to re-paint the screen after finishing one and before starting the next one. And we'll be able to see the slow but glorious transition from red to green to back, rather than meditating at the white screen for three seconds.

Interactive example and full code
https://advanced-react.com/examples/12/04

This is what React does for us. Essentially, it's a crazy complicated and very efficient engine that splits our giant, giant blobs of hundreds of npm dependencies combined with our own coding into the smallest possible chunks that browsers are able to process in under 13 ms (ideally).

Back to useEffect vs useLayoutEffect

Now, finally, back to `useEffect` vs `useLayoutEffect` and how to answer the questions we had at the beginning.

`useLayoutEffect` is something that React runs synchronously during component updates. In this code:

```
const Component = () => {
  useLayoutEffect(() => {
    // do something
  })

  return ...
}
```

Whatever we render inside the `Component` will be run with `useLayoutEffect` as the same "task". React guarantees this. Even if we update state inside `useLayoutEffect`, which we usually think of as an asynchronous task, React will still make sure that the entire flow is run synchronously.

If we return to the "navigation" example that we implemented at the beginning, from the browser's perspective, it would be just one "task".

useLayoutEffect

| Initial render | useLayoutEffect | state change | re-render | Hide invisible items |

This situation is exactly the same as the red-green-black border transition that we couldn't see!

The flow with `useEffect`, on the other hand, will be split into two tasks:

The first one renders the "initial" pass of navigation with all the buttons. The second one removes those children that we don't need. With screen re-painting in between! Exactly the same situation as with borders inside timeouts.

So to answer the questions we had at the beginning. Is it safe to use `useLayoutEffect`? Yep! Can it hurt performance? Absolutely! The last thing we need is for our entire React app to turn into one giant synchronous "task".

Use `useLayoutEffect` only when you need to get rid of the visual "glitches" caused by the need to adjust the UI according to the real sizes of elements. For everything else, `useEffect` is the way to go. And you might not even need that one either[15].

A bit more about useEffect

While the mental model of `useEffect` being run inside `setTimeout` is convenient to understand the difference, it's not technically correct. First of all, to make the implementation details clear, React uses a `postMessage` in combination with `requestAnimationFrame` trick[16] instead.

Second, it's not actually *guaranteed* to run asynchronously. While React will try to optimize it as much as possible, there are cases when it can run before the browser paint and block it as a result. One of those cases is when you already have `useLayoutEffect` somewhere in the chain of updates.

The thing is, React runs re-renders in "snapshots", or cycles. Every re-render cycle will look something like this, in this order: "State update triggered -> `useLayoutEffect` triggered -> `useEffect` triggered". If any of these trigger a state update, it will start another re-render cycle. But before doing that, React needs to *finish* the cycle that initiated the state update. So `useEffect` has to run before the new cycle starts. So if the state update is triggered inside `useLayoutEffect`, which is synchronous, React has no choice but to run `useEffect` synchronously as well.

useLayoutEffect in Next.js and other SSR frameworks

Enough with the low-level JavaScript and browser stuff, let's return to our production code. Because in "real life," all of this is not something we need to care about that often. In "real life," we'd want to just code our beautiful responsive navigation and build some nice user experience with it in some fancy framework like Next.js.

Howevver, when we try to do that, the first thing we'll notice is that *it doesn't freaking work*. Like at all. The glitching is still there, there is no magic anymore. To replicate it, just copy-paste our previously fixed navigation into your Next.js app, if you have one.

What's happening?

It's SSR. Server-side rendering. A cool feature that some frameworks support by default. And a real pain when it comes to things like this.

You see, when we have SSR enabled, the very first pass at rendering React components and calling all the lifecycle events is done on the server before the code reaches the browser. If you're not familiar with how SSR works, all it means is that somewhere on the backend, some method calls something like `React.renderToString(<App />)`. React then goes through all the components in the app, "renders" them (i.e., just calls their functions), and produces the HTML that these components represent.

```
const Component = ({ items }) => {
  return (
    <div className="navigation">
      {items.map((item) => (
        <a href={item.href}>{item.name}</a>
      ))}
    </div>
  )
}

const app = `
  <div className="navigation">
    <a href="/about">About us</a>
    <a href="/team">Team</a>
    <a href="/blog">Blog</a>
    <a href="/contact">Contact</a>
    <a href="/services">Services</a>
  </div>
`;
```

Then, this HTML is injected into the page that is going to be sent to the
browser, and off it goes. Just like in the good old times when everything
was generated on the server, and we used JavaScript only to open menus.
After that, the browser downloads the page, shows it to us, downloads all
the scripts (including React), runs them (including React again), React goes
through that pre-generated HTML, sprinkles some interactivity on it, and
our page is now alive again.

The problem here is: *there is no browser yet* when we generate that initial
HTML. So anything that would involve calculating actual sizes of elements
(like we do in our `useLayoutEffect`) will simply not work on the server:
there are no elements with dimensions yet, just strings. And since the whole
purpose of `useLayoutEffect` is to get access to the element's sizes,
there is not much point in running it on the server. And React doesn't.

As a result, what we see during the very first load when the browser shows
us the page that is not interactive yet is what we rendered during the "first
pass" stage in our component: the row of all the buttons, including the
"more" button. After the browser has a chance to execute everything and
React comes alive, it finally can run `useLayoutEffect`, and the buttons
are finally hidden. But the visual glitch is there.

How to fix it is a user experience problem and depends entirely on what
you're willing to show to your users "by default." We could show them some

"loading" state instead of the menu. Or show one or two of the most important menu items. Or even hide the items completely and only render them on the client. It's up to you.

One way to do it is just to introduce a "shouldRender" state variable and flip it to "true" in `useEffect`:

```
const Component = () => {
  const [shouldRender, setShouldRender] = useState(false);

  useEffect(() => {
    setShouldRender(true);
  }, []);

  if (!shouldRender) return <SomeNavigationSubstitude />;

  return <Navigation />;
};
```

`useEffect` will only run on the client, so the initial SSR pass will show us the substitute component. Then, the client code will kick in, `useEffect` will run, the state will change, and React will replace it with the normal responsive navigation.

Don't be afraid of introducing state here, and don't try to do conditional rendering like this:

```
const Component = () => {
  // Detectign SSR by checking whether window is there
  if (typeof window === undefined)
    return <SomeNavigationSubstitude />;

  return <Navigation />;
};
```

While technically `typeof window === undefined` would be an indication of the SSR environment (there is no window on the server), this will not work for our use case. React needs the HTML coming from SSR and from the first initial render on the client to match exactly. Otherwise, your app will behave like it's drunk: styles will be broken, blocks will be mispositioned, content will appear in weird places.

Key takeaways

That's all for the "flickering" for now. In the next chapter, we'll continue our conversation about the UI and learn how to deal with Portals and why. In the meantime, a few things to remember:

- When we calculate the dimensions of elements inside the `useEffect` hook and then hide them or adjust their size, we might see the visual "glitch".
- This is happening because normally `useEffect` is run asynchronously. Asynchronous code is a separate task from the browser's perspective. So it has a chance to paint the state "before" and "after" the change, resulting in the glitch.
- We can prevent this behavior with the `useLayoutEffect` hook. This hook is run synchronously. From the browser's perspective, it will be one large, unbreakable task. So the browser will wait and will not paint anything until the task is complete and the final dimensions are calculated.
- In the SSR environment, `useLayoutEffect` will not work since React doesn't run `useLayoutEffect` in SSR mode, and the "glitch" will be visible again.
- This can be fixed by opting out of SSR for this specific feature.

Chapter 13. React portals and why do we need them

Let's talk about UI some more. In the previous chapter, we solved the annoying "flickering" problem. Now, let's take a look at another fun UI bug: content clipping.

You might have heard that we need Portals in React to escape it when rendering elements inside elements with `overflow: hidden`. Every second article on the internet about Portals has this example. This is actually not true: we can escape content "clipping" with just pure CSS. We need Portals for other reasons. This "overflow problem" also might give a false sense of security: if we just don't have any `overflow: hidden` in the app, we can just easily position everything everywhere safely. Also not true.

Let's deep dive into all of this now and learn:

- How the CSS positioning of elements works.
- What Stacking Context is.
- How to escape content clipping with CSS.
- Why we can't do everything with CSS and need Portals.
- How Portals actually work and their caveats.

Just in case: this is a CSS-heavy chapter. The first half of it covers CSS-only concepts in detail, since not every React developer is proficient in CSS.

CSS: absolute positioning

Let's start with the simplest app and some basics that most people probably already know.

We have a page with some functionality and a button somewhere in the middle. When the button is clicked, I want to show some additional information:

```
const App = () => {
  const [isVisible, setIsVisible] = useState(false);

  return (
    <>
      <SomeComponent />
      <button onClick={() => setIsVisible(true)}>
        show more
      </button>
      {isVisible && <ModalDialog />}
      <AnotherComponent />
    </>
  );
};
```

With this implementation, the additional content, when it appears, will "push" the content from `AnotherComponent` down. This is the normal flow of any HTML document and the default behavior of "block" HTML elements: `div`, `p`, all `h` tags, etc.

But we want to implement the additional content as a modal dialog, and modal dialogs typically appear *on top* of the page content. What I want is for the `ModalDialog` component to be able to *escape* the normal document flow. The most common way to achieve that is through the CSS property "position"[17].

The `position` property supports two values that allow us to break away from the document flow: `absolute` and `fixed`. Let's start with `absolute` and try to implement the dialog using it. All we need to do is apply the `position: absolute` CSS to the div in the `ModalDialog` component:

```
// somewhere where you declare your css
.modal {
  position: absolute;
```

```
}

// our React component
const ModalDialog = () => {
  return (
    <div className="modal">
      some additional info
    </div>
  )
}
```

And voila! The content is no longer part of the document layout and appears at the top. Now I just need to position it correctly by setting some meaningful values in the `top` and `left` CSS properties. Assuming I want the dialog in the middle of the screen, the CSS for it would look something like this:

```
.modal {
  position: absolute;
  width: 300px;
  top: 100px;
  left: 50%;
  margin-left: -150px;
}
```

This dialog will appear in the middle of the screen, with a `100px` gap at the top.

Interactive example and full code
https://advanced-react.com/examples/13/01

So, technically, this works. But if you look at the existing dialogs in your app or any of the UI libraries, it's highly unlikely that they use `position: absolute` there. Or even tooltips, dropdown menus, or any UI element that pops up, really.

There are reasons for this.

Absolute is not that absolute

First of all, the absolute position is not exactly... absolute. It's actually relative: relative to the closest element with the `position` set to any value. In our case, it just works by accident: because I don't have any positioned elements between my modal dialog and the root of the app.

If the dialog happens to be rendered inside a div with `position: relative` (or `sticky` or `absolute`) and this div is not in the middle of the page, then it all falls apart. The modal will be positioned in the middle of that div, not in the middle of the screen.

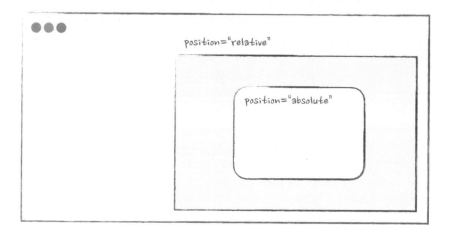

Interactive example and full code
https://advanced-react.com/examples/13/02

Okay, so for elements that are supposed to be positioned relative to the screen, the `absolute` position is not the best choice. Although it's still possible to calculate, of course, just not with pure CSS.

But what about something like a tooltip or a dropdown menu? Those we would expect to be positioned relative to the element they originate from, isn't it? So the fact that absolute is relative is perfect for that: we can just use `offsetLeft` and `offsetTop` on the trigger to get the left/top distance between the trigger and the parent, and our dialog/tooltip/menu will position itself relative to the trigger all the time perfectly.

And technically, yes, it will work.

Until Stacking Context rules kick in.

Understanding Stacking Context

The Stacking Context[18] is a nightmare for anyone who has ever tried to use `z-index` on positioned elements. The Stacking Context is a three-dimensional way of looking at our HTML elements. It's like a Z-axis, in addition to our normal X and Y dimensions (window width and height), that defines what sits on top of what when an element is rendered on the screen. If an element has a shadow, for example, that overlaps with surrounding elements, should the shadow be rendered on top of them or underneath them? This is determined by the Stacking Context.

The default rules of the Stacking Context are quite complicated by themselves. Normally, elements are stacked in the order of their appearance in the DOM. In code like this:

```
<div>grey</div>
<div>red</div>
<div>green</div>
```

The green div is after the red, so it will be "in front" from the Stacking Context rules point of view, and the red will be in front of the grey. If I add a small negative margin to them, we'll see this picture:

Elements with the `position` set to `absolute` or `relative`, however, will always be pushed forward. If I just add `position: relative` to the red div, the green suddenly appears under it.

```
<div>grey</div>
<div style={{ position: "relative" }}>red</div>
<div>green</div>
```

For our absolutely positioned dialog, that would mean that if it's inside the red div, with the position set, it will be okay and on top of everything. But if it's inside the grey div, then the *red div will be on top of the dialog*.

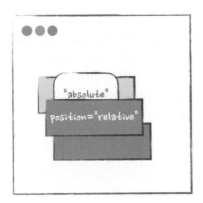

To fix this situation, we have the `z-index` CSS property. This property allows us to manipulate that Z-axis within the same Stacking Context. By default, it's zero. So if I set the `z-index` of the dialog to a negative value, it will appear behind all the divs. If set to positive, then it will appear on top of all the divs.

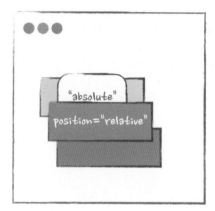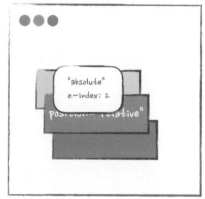

Within the same Stacking Context is the key here. If something creates a new Stacking Context, that `z-index` will be relative to the new context. It's a completely isolated bubble. The new Stacking Context will be controlled as its own isolated black box by the rules of the parent Context, and what happens inside stays inside.

The combination of `position` and `z-index` on the same element will create its own Stacking Context. From our colorful divs' point of view, that would mean that if I add `position: relative; z-index: 1` to the grey div and `position: relative; z-index: 2` to the red div, both of them will be parents of their own Stacking Contexts. The grey div and everything inside it will be "underneath" the red one, including our modal dialog. Even if I change the `z-index` on the dialog to the magic `9999` number, it won't matter: the dialog will still appear under the red div.

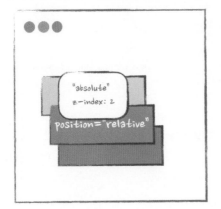
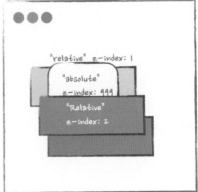

Play around with the `z-index` on the grey div in the code example below; it's truly fascinating. If I remove it, the new Stacking Context disappears, and the dialog is now part of the global context and its rules and starts appearing on top of the red div. As soon as I add a `z-index` to the grey div that is less than the red div, it moves underneath.

And it's not only the combination of `position` and `z-index` that triggers it, by the way. The `transform` property will do it. So any of your leftover CSS animations have the potential to mess the positioned elements up. Or `z-index` on Flex or Grid children. Or a bunch of other different properties[19].

Interactive example and full code
https://advanced-react.com/examples/13/03

And, of course, finally, the elements with `overflow` . By the way, just setting `overflow` on an element won't clip the absolutely positioned div inside; it needs to be in combination with `position: relative` . But yeah, if an absolutely positioned dialog is rendered inside the div with `overflow` and `position` , then it will be clipped.

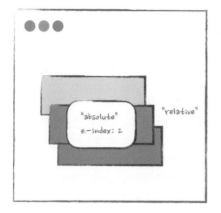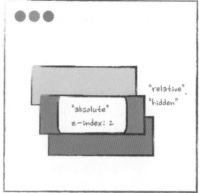

Interactive example and full code
https://advanced-react.com/examples/13/04

Can we do something about all of this? Yep, of course. Partially. We can fix the overflow problem in no time at least.

Position: fixed. Escape the overflow

There is another `position` value that we can use to escape the normal document flow: the `fixed` value. It's similar to `absolute`, only it positions the elements not relative to their positioned parents but relative to the viewport. For something like the modal dialog that should be positioned in the middle of the screen, regardless of the parents, this value is much more beneficial.

Also, since it's positioned relative to the screen, this `position` actually allows us to escape the `overflow` trap. So, *in theory*, we could have used it for our dialogs and tooltips.

However, even `position: fixed` cannot escape the rules of the Stacking Context. Nothing can. It's like a black hole: as soon as it forms, everything within its gravitational reach is gone. No one gets out.

If the grey div has `z-index: 1` and the red div is with `z-index: 2` - it's game over for modals. They will appear underneath.

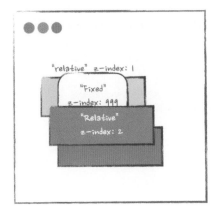 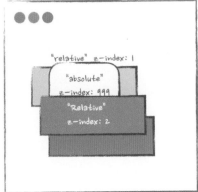

Interactive example and full code
https://advanced-react.com/examples/13/05

Another issue with `position: fixed` is that it's not *always* positioned relative to the viewport. It's actually positioned relative to what is known as the Containing Block. It just happens to be the viewport most of the time. Unless some of the parents have certain properties set, then it will be positioned relative to that parent. And we'll have the same situation we had at the very beginning with `position: absolute`.

Properties that trigger the forming of the new Containing Block[20] for `position: fixed` are relatively rare, but they include `transform`, and that one is widely used for animation.

Stacking Context in real apps

Okay, all of this is really fun but a bit theoretical. Would a situation like the Stacking Context trap even happen in a real app? Of course! And quite easily, actually.

The prime candidates are all sorts of animations or "sticky" blocks like headers or columns. Those are the most likely places where we'd be forced to set either `position` with `z-index`, or `translate`. And those will form a new Stacking Context.

Just open a few of your favorite popular websites that have "sticky" elements or animations, open Chrome Dev Tools, find some block deep in the DOM tree, set its position to `fixed` with a high `z-index`, and move it around a bit. Just for the fun of it, I checked Facebook, Airbnb, Gmail, OpenAI, and LinkedIn. On three of those, the main area is a trap: any block with `position: fixed` and `z-index: 9999` within it will appear *underneath* the sticky header.

There is only one way to escape from that trap: to make sure that the modal is not rendered inside the DOM elements that form the Stacking Context. In the world without React, we'd just append that modal to the body or some div at the root of the app with something like:

```
const modalDialog = ... // get the dialog where the button is clicked
document.getElementByClassName('body')[0].appendChild(modalDialog);
```

In React, we can escape that Stacking Context trap with the tool called Portal. Finally, time to do React!

How React Portal can solve this

Let's recreate the trap in something more interesting than a bunch of colorful divs just to make our code more realistic and to see how easily it can happen. And then fix it for good.

Let's do a very simple app: a header with `position: sticky`, the "collapsible" navigation on the left, and the modal dialog inside our main area.

```
const App = () => {
  const [isVisible, setIsVisible] = useState(false);
```

```
  return (
    <>
      <div className="header"></div>
      <div className="layout">
        <div className="sidebar">// some links here</div>
        <div className="main">
          <button onClick={() => setIsVisible(true)}>
            show more
          </button>
          {isVisible && <ModalDialog />}
        </div>
      </div>
    </>
  );
};
```

Our header is going to be sticky, so I'll set the sticky position for it:

```
.header {
  position: sticky;
}
```

And I want our navigation to move into the "collapsed" state smoothly, without any jumping or disappearing blocks. So I'll set the `transition` property on it and the main area:

```
.main {
  transition: all 0.3s ease-in;
}

.sidebar {
  transition: all 0.3s ease-in;
}
```

And translate them to the left when the navigation is collapsed and back when it's expanded:

```
const App = () => {
  // hold navigation state here
```

```
  const [isNavExpanded, setIsNavExpanded] = useState(true);

  return (
    <>
      <div className="header"></div>
      <div className="layout">
        <div
          className="sidebar"
          // translate the nav to the left if collapsed, and back
          style={{
            transform: isNavExpanded
              ? 'translate(0, 0)'
              : 'translate(-300px, 0)',
          }}
        >
          ...
        </div>
        <div
          className="main"
          // translate the main to the left if nav is collapsed, and
back
          style={{
            transform: isNavExpanded
              ? 'translate(0, 0)'
              : 'translate(-300px, 0)',
          }}
        >
          {/*main here*/}
        </div>
      </div>
    </>
  );
};
```

That already works beautifully, except for one thing: when I scroll, the
header disappears under the sidebar and the main area. That's no problem,
I already know how to deal with it: just need to set `z-index: 2` for the
header. Done, and now the header is always on top, and expand/collapse
works like a charm!

Interactive example and full code
https://advanced-react.com/examples/13/06

Except for one thing: the modal dialog in the main area is now completely busted. It used to be positioned in the middle of the screen, but not anymore. And when I scroll with it open, it appears under the header. Everything in the code is reasonable, there are no random `position: relative` , and still, that happened. The Stacking Context trap.

In order to fix it, we need to render the modal dialog outside of our main area. In our simple app, we could just move it to the bottom, of course: the button, state, and dialog are within the same component. In the real world, it's not going to be that simple. More likely than not, the button will be buried deep inside the render tree, and propagating state up will be a massive pain and performance killer. Context could help, but it has its own caveats.

Instead, we can use the `createPortal` function that React gives us. Well, technically, the `react-dom` library, but it only matters for the import path in our case. It accepts two arguments:

- **What** we want to teleport in the form of a React Element (our `<ModalDialog />`)
- **Where** we want to teleport it to in the form of a *DOM element*. Not an `id` , but the element itself! We would have to refresh our rusty JavaScript skills for this and write something like `document.getElementById("root")` .

```
import { createPortal } from 'react-dom';

const App = () => {
  return (
    <>
        ... // the rest of the code with the button
      {isVisible &&
        createPortal(
          <ModalDialog />,
          document.getElementById('root'),
```

```
      )}
    </>
  );
};
```

That's it, the trap is no more! We still "render" the dialog together with the button from our developer experience perspective. But it ends up inside the element with `id="root"`. If you open Chrome Developer Tools, you'll see it right at the bottom of it.

Interactive example and full code
https://advanced-react.com/examples/13/07

And the dialog is now centered, as it's supposed to be, and appears on top of the header, as it should.

But what are the consequences of doing that? What about re-renders, React lifecycle, events, access to Context, etc.? Easy. The rules of teleportation in React are:

- What happens in React stays in React.
- Where React has no power, the behavior is controlled by the DOM rules.

What does this mean exactly?

React lifecycle, re-renders, Context, and Portals

From a React perspective, this modal dialog is part of the render tree of the component that created the `<ModalDialog />` element. In our case, the `App` component. If I trigger the **re-render** of the `App`, all components rendered inside of it will re-render, including our dialog, if it's open.

If our `App` has access to **Context**, the dialog will have access to exactly the same Context.

If the part of the app where the dialog is created **unmounts**, the dialog will also disappear.

If I want to intercept a **click event** that happens in the modal, the `onClick` handler on the "main" div will be able to do that. "Click" here is part of synthetic events, so they "bubble" through the React tree, not the regular DOM tree. Same story with any synthetic events that React manages[21].

> **Interactive example and full code**
> https://advanced-react.com/examples/13/08

CSS, native JavaScript, form submit, and Portals

From the DOM perspective, this dialog is no longer part of the "main" app. So everything that is DOM-related will change.

If you rely on CSS inheritance and cascading to style the dialog in the "main" part, it won't work anymore.

```
// won't work with portalled modal
.main .dialog {
  background: red;
}
```

If you rely on "native" events propagation, it also won't work. If, instead of the `onClick` callback on the "main" div, you try to catch events that originated in the modal via `element.addEventListener`, it won't work.

```
const App = () => {
```

```
  const ref = useRef(null);

  useEffect(() => {
    const el = ref.current;

    el.addEventListener("click", () => {
      // trying to catch events, originated in the portalled modal
      // not going to work!!
    });
  }, []);

  // the rest of the app
  return <div ref={ref} ... />
}
```

If you try to grab the parent of the modal via `parentElement` , it will return the `root` div, not the main app. And the same story with any native JavaScript functions that operate on the DOM elements.

And finally, `onSubmit` on `<form>` elements. This is the least obvious thing about this. It *feels* the same as `onClick` , but in reality, the *submit event is not managed by React*[22]. It's a native API and DOM elements thing. If I wrap the main part of the app in `<form>` , then clicking on the buttons inside the dialog won't trigger the "submit" event! From the DOM perspective, those buttons are outside of the form. If you want to have a form inside the dialog and want to rely on the `onSubmit` callback, then the `form` tag should be inside the dialog as well.

> **Interactive example and full code**
> https://advanced-react.com/examples/13/09

Key takeaways

That's enough about CSS and portalling for the book, I think. Things to remember next time you're trying to position elements:

- `position: absolute` positions an element relative to a positioned parent.
- `position: fixed` positions an element relative to the viewport unless a new Containing Block is formed.
- `position: absolute` elements will be clipped inside the `overflow: hidden` elements.
- `position: fixed` elements can escape the `overflow: hidden` problem, but they can't escape the Stacking Context.
- Nothing can escape the Stacking Context. If you are trapped there, it's game over.
- Stacking Context is formed by setting `position` and `z-index`, by setting `translate`, and so many other things.
- Portals allow you to easily render some elements, like modal dialogs, outside of their current DOM position so that the Stacking Context doesn't trap them.
- When using Portals, the rules are:
    - What happens in React stays within the React hierarchy.
    - What happens outside of React follows DOM structure rules.

Chapter 14. Data fetching on the client and performance

Performance in React is not only about re-renders. No instantaneous re-renders will save you if fetching the main data takes two seconds. Or if the page is so "junky" while it fetches data that it causes a headache for your users from all the UI elements moving and spinners spinning. Fetching data in the frontend world is hard, and React is no exception, unfortunately.

Have you tried recently to wrap your head around what the latest on data fetching is? The chaos of endless data management libraries, GraphQL or not GraphQL, `useEffect` is evil since it causes waterfalls, `Suspense` is supposed to save the world, but at the moment of publishing this book, it is still not officially ready for data fetching. And then the patterns like `fetch-on-render`, `fetch-then-render`, and `render-as-you-fetch` that confuse even people who write about them sometimes. What on Earth is going on? Why do I suddenly need a PhD to just make a simple GET request?

And what is the actual "right way" to fetch data in React? In this chapter, you'll learn:

- Types of data fetching on the Frontend.
- Can we use just a simple `fetch` for data fetching?
- What do we mean by a "performant" app?
- What are the browser limitations when it comes to fetching data?
- What request waterfalls are and how they appear?
- A few solutions to the request waterfalls problem.

Types of data fetching

Generally speaking, in the modern frontend world, we can loosely separate the concept of "data fetching" into two categories: initial data fetching and data fetching on demand.

Data on demand is something that you fetch after a user interacts with a page in order to update their experience. All the various autocompletes, dynamic forms, and search experiences fall under this category. In React, the fetch of this data is usually triggered in callbacks.

Initial data is the data you'd expect to see on a page right away when you open it. It's the data we need to fetch before a component ends up on the screen. It's something that we need to be able to show users some meaningful experience as soon as possible. In React, if no SSR is involved, fetching data like this usually happens in `useEffect` (or in `componentDidMount` for class components).

Interestingly enough, although these concepts seem totally different, the core principles and fundamental patterns of data fetching are exactly the same for both. However, initial data fetching is usually the most crucial for the majority of people. During this stage, the first impression of your apps as "slow as hell" or "blazing fast" will form. That's why the rest of the chapter will focus solely on initial data fetching and how to do it properly with performance in mind.

Do I really need an external library to fetch data in React?

First things first. External libraries for data fetching in React - yes or no?

Short answer - no. And yes. Depends on your use case. If you actually just need to fetch a bit of data once and forget about it, then no, you don't need anything. A simple `fetch` in the `useEffect` hook will do just fine:

```
const Component = () => {
  const [data, setData] = useState();

  useEffect(() => {
```

```
// fetch data
const dataFetch = async () => {
  const data = await (
    await fetch(
      'https://run.mocky.io/v3/b3bcb9d2-d8e9-43c5-bfb7-
0062c85be6f9',
    )
  ).json();

  // set state when the data received
  setData(data);
};

dataFetch();
}, []);

return <>...</>;
};
```

But as soon as your use case exceeds "fetch once and forget," you're going to face tough questions. What about error handling? What if multiple components want to fetch data from this exact endpoint? Should I cache that data? For how long? What about race conditions? What if I want to remove the component from the screen? Should I cancel this request? What about memory leaks? And so on and so forth.

Not a single question from that list is even React-specific; it's a general problem of fetching data over the network. To solve these problems (and more!), there are only two paths: you either need to reinvent the wheel and write a lot of code to solve these. Or rely on some existing library that has been doing this for years.

Some libraries, like Axios[23], will abstract some concerns, like canceling requests, but will have no opinion on React-specific API. Others, like swr[24], will handle pretty much everything for you, including caching. But essentially, the choice of technology doesn't matter much here. No library or Suspense in the world can improve the performance of your app just by itself. They just make some things easier at the cost of making some things harder. You **always** need to understand the fundamentals of data fetching and data orchestration patterns and techniques in order to write performant apps.

What is a "performant" React app?

Before jumping into concrete patterns and code examples, let's have a conversation about what "performance" of an app is. How do you know whether an app is "performant"? It's relatively straightforward with a simple component: you just measure how long it takes to render it, and voila! The smaller the number, the more "performant" (i.e., faster) your component is.

With async operations, which data fetching typically is, and in the context of large apps and the user experience point of view, it's not that obvious.

Imagine we are implementing an issue view for an issue tracker. It would have sidebar navigation on the left with a bunch of links, the main issue information in the center - things like title, description, or assignee, and a section with comments underneath that.

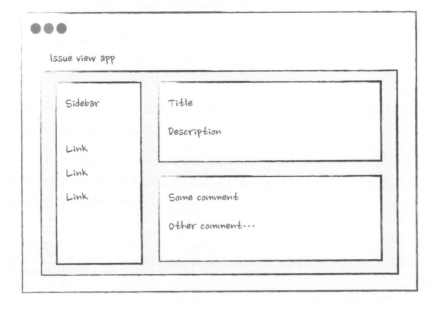

And let's say the app is implemented in three different ways:

1. Shows a loading state until all the data is loaded, and then renders everything in one go. Takes ~3 seconds.

2. Shows a loading state until sidebar data is loaded first, renders sidebar, and keeps loading state until the data is finished in the main part. The sidebar to appear takes ~1 second, the rest of the app appears in ~3 seconds. Overall, it takes ~4 seconds.

3. Shows a loading state until the main issue data is loaded, then renders it, keeps the loading state for sidebar and comments. When sidebar loaded - renders it, comments are still in the loading state. The main part appears in ~2 seconds, the sidebar in ~1 second after that, it takes another ~2 seconds for the comments to appear. Overall takes ~5s to appear.

Interactive example and full code for the App 1
https://advanced-react.com/examples/14/01

Interactive example and full code for the App 2
https://advanced-react.com/examples/14/02

Interactive example and full code for the App 3
https://advanced-react.com/examples/14/03

Which app is the most performant here? What do you think?

And the answer is, of course, tricky, and the most performant app is not the one that you chose, but... None of them. Or all of them. Or any of them. *It depends.*

The **first app** loads in just 3 seconds - the fastest of them all. From a pure numbers perspective, it's a clear winner. But it doesn't show anything to users for 3 seconds - the longest of them all. Clear loser?

The **second app** loads something on the screen (Sidebar) in just 1 second. From the perspective of showing at least something as fast as possible, it's a clear winner. But it's the longest of them all to show the main part of the issue. Clear loser?

The **third app** loads the Issue information first. From the perspective of showing the main piece of the app first, it's a clear winner. But the "natural" flow of information for left-to-right languages is from the top-left to the bottom-right. This is how we usually read. This app violates it, and it makes the experience the most "junky" one here. Not to mention it's the longest of them all to load. Clear loser?

It **always** depends on the message you're trying to convey to the users. Think of yourself as a storyteller, and the app is your story. What is the most important piece of the story? What is the second? Does your story have a flow? Can you even tell it in pieces, or do you want your users to see the story in full right away, without any intermediate steps?

When, and only when, you have an idea of what your story should look like, then it will be time to assemble the app and optimize the story to be as fast as possible. And the true power comes here not from various libraries, GraphQL, or Suspense, but from the knowledge of:

- when is it okay to start fetching data?
- what can we do while the data fetching is in progress?
- what should we do when the data fetching is done?

and knowing a few techniques that allow you to control all three stages of the data fetching requests.

But before jumping into actual techniques, we need to understand two more very fundamental things: the React lifecycle and browser resources and their influence on our goal.

React lifecycle and data fetching

The most important thing to know and remember when planning your fetch requests strategy is when the React component's lifecycle is triggered. We already covered conditional rendering in *Chapter 3. Configuration concerns with elements as props*, but it's worth repeating here. Check out this code:

```
const Child = () => {
  useEffect(() => {
    // do something here, like fetching data for the Child
  }, []);

  return <div>Some child</div>;
};

const Parent = () => {
  // set loading to true initially
  const [isLoading, setIsLoading] = useState(true);

  if (isLoading) return 'loading';

  return <Child />;
};
```

We have our `Parent` component, which conditionally renders the `Child` component based on state. Will the Child's `useEffect`, and therefore the fetch request there, be triggered? The intuitive answer is the correct one - it won't. *Only* after Parent's `isLoading` state changes to `false`, will the rendering and all other effects be triggered in the `Child` component.

What about this code for the `Parent`:

```
const Parent = () => {
  // set loading to true initially
  const [isLoading, setIsLoading] = useState(true);

  // child is now here! before return
  const child = <Child />;
```

```
  if (isLoading) return 'loading';

  return child;
};
```

The functionality is the same: if `isLoading` is set to `false`, show `Child`, if `true` - show the loading state. But the `<Child />` element this time is before the if condition. Will the `useEffect` in `Child` be triggered this time? And the answer is now less intuitive, and I've seen a lot of people stumble here. The answer is still the same - no, it won't.

When we write `const child = <Child />`, we don't "render" the `Child` component. `<Child />` is nothing more than syntax sugar for a function that creates a *description* of a future element. It is only rendered when this description ends up in the actual visible render tree - i.e., returned from the component. Until then, it just sits there idly as an object and does nothing.

There are more things to know about the React lifecycle, of course: the order in which all of this is triggered, what is triggered before or after painting, what slows down what and how, the `useLayoutEffect` hook, etc. But all of this becomes relevant much later, when you have orchestrated everything perfectly and are now fighting for milliseconds in a very big, complicated app.

Browser limitations and data fetching

You might be thinking at this point, "Gosh, it's so complicated. Can't we just fire all the requests as soon as possible, shove that data in some global store, and then just use it when it's available? Why even bother with the lifecycle and orchestration of anything?"

I feel you. And sure, we can do it if the app is simple and only has a few requests to make ever. But in large apps, where we can have dozens of data fetching requests, that strategy can backfire. And I'm not even talking about server load and whether it can handle it. Let's assume that it can. The problem is that our browsers can't!

Did you know that browsers have a limit on how many requests in parallel to the same host they can handle? Assuming the server is HTTP1 (which is still 70% of the internet), the number is not that big. In Chrome, it's just 6[25]. 6 requests in parallel! If you fire more at the same time, all the rest of them will have to queue and wait for the first available "slot."

And 6 requests for initial data fetching in a large app is not unreasonable. Our very simple "issue tracker" already has three, and we haven't even implemented anything of value yet. Imagine all the angry looks you'll get if you just add a somewhat slow analytics request that literally does nothing at the very beginning of the app, and it ends up slowing down the entire experience.

Want to see it in action? Here's the simplest code:

```
const App = () => {
  // I extracted fetching and useEffect into a hook
  const { data } = useData('/fetch-some-data');

  if (!data) return 'loading...';

  return <div>I'm an app</div>;
};
```

Assume that the fetch request is super fast there, taking just ~50ms. If I add just six requests before that app that take 10 seconds, without waiting for them or resolving them, the whole app load will take those 10 seconds (in Chrome, of course).

```
// no waiting, no resolving, just fetch and drop it
fetch('https://some-url.com/url1');
fetch('https://some-url.com/url2');
fetch('https://some-url.com/url3');
fetch('https://some-url.com/url4');
fetch('https://some-url.com/url5');
fetch('https://some-url.com/url6');

const App = () => {
  ... same app code
```

```
}
```

Interactive example and full code
https://advanced-react.com/examples/14/04

Requests waterfalls: how they appear

Finally, it's time to do some serious coding! Now that we have all the needed moving pieces and know how they fit together, it's time to write the story of our issue tracking app. Let's implement those examples from the beginning of the chapter and see what is possible.

Let's start by laying out components first, then wire the data fetching afterward. We'll have the app component itself, which will render Sidebar and Issue, and Issue will render Comments.

```
const App = () => {
  return (
    <>
      <Sidebar />
      <Issue />
    </>
  );
};

const Sidebar = () => {
  return; // some sidebar links
};

const Issue = () => {
  return (
    <>
      // some issue data
      <Comments />
    </>
  );
};
```

```
const Comments = () => {
  return; // some issue comments
};
```

Now to the data fetching. Let's first extract the actual fetch and useEffect and state management into a nice hook to simplify the examples:

```
export const useData = (url) => {
  const [state, setState] = useState();

  useEffect(() => {
    const dataFetch = async () => {
      const data = await (await fetch(url)).json();

      setState(data);
    };

    dataFetch();
  }, [url]);

  return { data: state };
};
```

Then, I would probably naturally want to co-locate fetching requests with the large components: issue data in `Issue` and comments list in `Comments`. And would want to show the loading state while we're waiting, of course!

```
const Comments = () => {
  // fetch is triggered in useEffect there, as normal
  const { data } = useData('/get-comments');

  // show loading state while waiting for the data
  if (!data) return 'loading';

  // rendering comments now that we have access to them!
  return data.map((comment) => <div>{comment.title}</div>);
};
```

And exactly the same code for `Issue` , only it will render the `Comments` component after loading:

```
const Issue = () => {
  // fetch is triggered in useEffect there, as normal
  const { data } = useData('/get-issue');

  // show loading state while waiting for the data
  if (!data) return 'loading';

  // render actual issue now that the data is here!
  return (
    <div>
      <h3>{data.title}</h3>
      <p>{data.description}</p>
      <Comments />
    </div>
  );
};
```

And the app itself:

```
const App = () => {
  // fetch is triggered in useEffect there, as normal
  const { data } = useData('/get-sidebar');

  // show loading state while waiting for the data
  if (!data) return 'loading';

  return (
    <>
      <Sidebar data={data} />
      <Issue />
    </>
  );
};
```

Boom, done!

There is only one small problem here. The app is terribly slow. Slower than all our examples from above!

What we did here is implement a classic waterfall of requests. Remember the React lifecycle part? Only components that are actually returned will be mounted, rendered, and as a result, will trigger useEffect and data fetching in it. In our case, every single component returns a "loading" state while it waits for data. And only when data is loaded does it switch to a component next in the render tree, triggers its own data fetching, returns a "loading" state, and the cycle repeats itself.

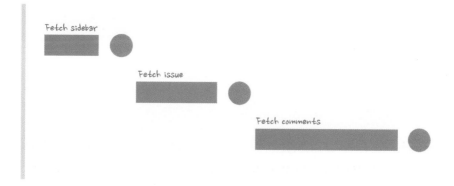

Waterfalls like that are not the best solution when you need to show the app as quickly as possible. Luckily, there are a few ways to deal with them (but not Suspense, about that one later).

How to solve requests waterfall

Promise.all solution

The first and easiest solution is to pull all of those data-fetching requests as high in the render tree as possible. In our case, it's our root component

App . But there is a catch: you can't just "move" them and leave it as is. We can't just do something like this:

```
useEffect(async () => {
  const sidebar = await fetch('/get-sidebar');
  const issue = await fetch('/get-issue');
  const comments = await fetch('/get-comments');
}, []);
```

This is just yet another waterfall, only co-located in a single component. We fetch sidebar data, await for it, then fetch the issue, await, fetch comments, await. The time when all the data will be available for rendering will be the sum of all those waiting times: 1s + 2s + 3s = 6 seconds. Instead, we need to fire them all *at the same time*, so that they are sent in parallel. That way, we will be waiting for all of them no longer than the longest of them: 3 seconds. 50% performance improvement!

One way to do it is to use `Promise.all` [26]:

```
useEffect(async () => {
  const [sidebar, issue, comments] = await Promise.all([
    fetch('/get-sidebar'),
    fetch('/get-issue'),
    fetch('/get-comments'),
  ]);
}, []);
```

and then save all of them to state in the parent component and pass them down to the children components as props:

```
const useAllData = () => {
  const [sidebar, setSidebar] = useState();
  const [comments, setComments] = useState();
  const [issue, setIssue] = useState();

  useEffect(() => {
    const dataFetch = async () => {
      // waiting for allthethings in parallel
      const result = (
```

```
        await Promise.all([
          fetch(sidebarUrl),
          fetch(issueUrl),
          fetch(commentsUrl),
        ])
      ).map((r) => r.json());

      // and waiting a bit more - fetch API is cumbersome
      const [sidebarResult, issueResult, commentsResult] =
        await Promise.all(result);

      // when the data is ready, save it to state
      setSidebar(sidebarResult);
      setIssue(issueResult);
      setComments(commentsResult);
    };

    dataFetch();
  }, []);

  return { sidebar, comments, issue };
};

const App = () => {
  // all the fetches were triggered in parallel
  const { sidebar, comments, issue } = useAllData();

  // show loading state while waiting for all the data
  if (!sidebar || !comments || !issue) return 'loading';

  // render the actual app here and pass data from state to children
  return (
    <>
      <Sidebar data={state.sidebar} />
      <Issue
        comments={state.comments}
        issue={state.issue}
      />
    </>
  );
};
```

This is how the very first app from the test at the beginning is implemented.

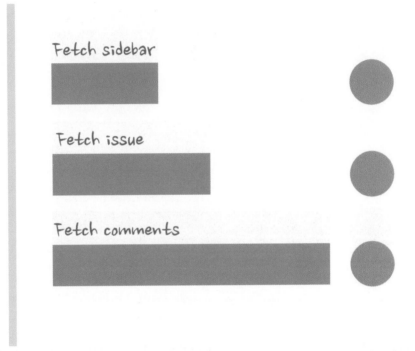

Parallel promises solution

But what if we don't want to wait for them all? Our comments are the slowest and the least important part of the page. It doesn't make much sense to block the rendering of the sidebar while we're waiting for them. Can we fire all requests in parallel, but wait for them independently?

Of course! We just need to transform those `fetch` from `async/await` syntax to proper old-fashioned promises[27] and save the data inside the `then` callback:

```
fetch('/get-sidebar')
```

```
  .then((data) => data.json())
  .then((data) => setSidebar(data));
fetch('/get-issue')
  .then((data) => data.json())
  .then((data) => setIssue(data));
fetch('/get-comments')
  .then((data) => data.json())
  .then((data) => setComments(data));
```

Now, every fetch request is fired in parallel but resolved independently. And now in the App's render, we can do pretty cool things, like render `Sidebar` and `Issue` as soon as their data ends up in the state:

```
const App = () => {
  const { sidebar, issue, comments } = useAllData();

  // show loading state while waiting for sidebar
  if (!sidebar) return 'loading';

  // render sidebar as soon as its data is available
  // but show loading state instead of issue and comments while we're
waiting for them
  return (
    <>
      <Sidebar data={sidebar} />
      {/*render local loading state for issue here if its data not
available*/}
      {/*inside Issue component we'd have to render 'loading' for
empty comments as well*/}
      {issue ? <Issue comments={comments} issue={issue} /> :
'loading''}
    </>
  )
}
```

Here, we render `Sidebar`, `Issue`, and `Comments` components as soon as their data becomes available - exactly the same behavior as the initial waterfall. But since we fired those requests in parallel, the overall waiting time will drop from 6 seconds to just 3 seconds. We just massively improved the performance of the app while keeping its behavior intact!

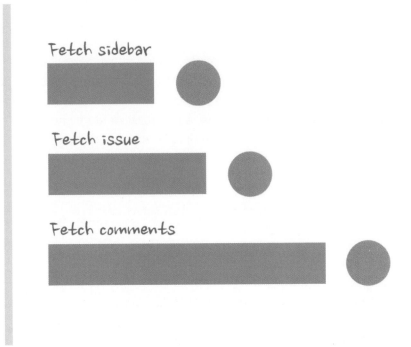

One thing to note here is that in this solution, we're triggering state change three times independently, which will cause three re-renders of the parent component. And considering that it's happening at the top of the app, unnecessary re-render like this might cause half of the app to re-render unnecessarily. The performance impact really depends on the order of your components, of course, and how big they are, but it's something to keep in mind.

Data providers to abstract away fetching

Lifting data loading up like in the examples above, although good for performance, is terrible for app architecture and code readability. Suddenly, instead of nicely co-located data fetching requests and their components, we have one giant component that fetches everything and massive props drilling throughout the entire app.

Fortunately, there is an easy(ish) solution to this: we can introduce the concept of "data providers" to the app. "Data provider" here would be just an abstraction around data fetching that gives us the ability to fetch data in one place of the app and access that data in another, bypassing all components in between. Essentially, it's like a mini-caching layer per request. In "raw" React, it's just a simple context:

```
const Context = React.createContext();

export const CommentsDataProvider = ({ children }) => {
  const [comments, setComments] = useState();

  useEffect(async () => {
    fetch('/get-comments')
      .then((data) => data.json())
      .then((data) => setComments(data));
  }, []);

  return (
    <Context.Provider value={comments}>
      {children}
    </Context.Provider>
  );
};

export const useComments = () => useContext(Context);
```

Exactly the same logic for all three of our requests. And then our monster App component turns into something as simple as this:

```
const App = () => {
  const sidebar = useSidebar();
  const issue = useIssue();

  // show loading state while waiting for sidebar
  if (!sidebar) return 'loading';
```

```
  // no more props drilling for any of those
  return (
    <>
      <Sidebar />
      {issue ? <Issue /> : 'loading''}
    </>
  )
}
```

Our three providers will wrap the `App` component and will fire fetching requests as soon as they are mounted in parallel:

```
export const VeryRootApp = () => {
  return (
    <SidebarDataProvider>
      <IssueDataProvider>
        <CommentsDataProvider>
          <App />
        </CommentsDataProvider>
      </IssueDataProvider>
    </SidebarDataProvider>
  );
};
```

And then in something like `Comments` (i.e., far, far deep into the render tree from the root app), we'll just access that data from "data provider":

```
const Comments = () => {
  // Look! No props drilling!
  const comments = useComments();
};
```

Interactive example and full code
https://advanced-react.com/examples/14/08

If you're not a huge fan of Context - not to worry, exactly the same concept will work with any state management solution of your choosing.

What if I fetch data before React?

One final trick to learn about fighting waterfalls. That one is very important to know so you can stop your colleagues from using it during PR reviews. What I'm trying to say is that it's a very dangerous thing to do, so use it wisely.

Let's take a look at our Comments component from when we implemented the very first waterfall, the one that was fetching data by itself (I moved the `getData` hook inside).

```
const Comments = () => {
  const [data, setData] = useState();

  useEffect(() => {
    const dataFetch = async () => {
      const data = await (
        await fetch('/get-comments')
      ).json();

      setData(data);
    };

    dataFetch();
  }, [url]);

  if (!data) return 'loading';

  return data.map((comment) => <div>{comment.title}</div>);
};
```

Pay special attention to the 6th line there. What is `fetch('/get-comments')`? It's nothing more than just a promise that we await inside our `useEffect`. It doesn't depend on anything of React in this case - no props, state, or internal variable dependencies. So, what will happen if I move it to the very top, before I even declare the `Comments` component? And then just `await` that promise inside the `useEffect` hook?

```
const commentsPromise = fetch('/get-comments');
```

```
const Comments = () => {
  useEffect(() => {
    const dataFetch = async () => {
      // just await the variable here
      const data = await (await commentsPromise).json();

      setState(data);
    };

    dataFetch();
  }, [url]);
};
```

A really fancy thing: our fetch call essentially "escapes" all React lifecycle and will be fired as soon as JavaScript is loaded on the page, before any of the `useEffect` anywhere is called. Even before the very first request in the root `App` component is called. It will be fired, JavaScript will move on to other things to process, and the data will just sit there quietly until someone actually resolves it. Which is what we're doing in our `useEffect` in `Comments`.

Remember our initial waterfall pic?

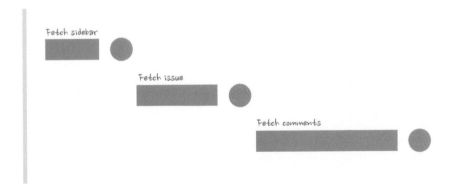

Just moving the fetch call outside of `Comments` resulted in this instead:

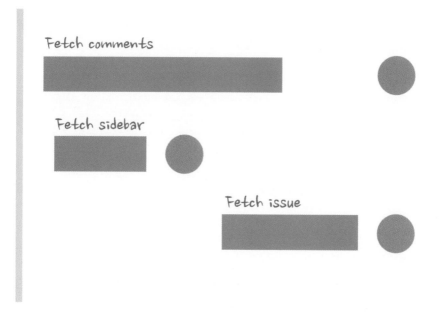

Interactive example and full code
https://advanced-react.com/examples/14/09

Technically speaking, we could've just moved all of our promises outside of
components, and that would've solved the waterfalls, and we wouldn't have
to deal with lifting fetching up or data providers.

So why didn't we? And why it's not a very common pattern?

Easy. Remember the **Browsers limitation** part? Only 6 requests in
parallel, the next one will queue. And fetches like these will be fired
immediately and completely uncontrollably. A component that fetches
heavy data and is rendered once in a blue moon, in your app with a
"traditional" waterfall approach, won't bother anyone until it's actually
rendered. But with this hack, it has the potential to steal the most valuable
milliseconds of initial fetching of critical data. And good luck to anyone
who's trying to figure out how a component that sits in some existential
corner of the code and is never even rendered on a screen can slow down
the entire app.

There are only two "legit" use cases that I can think of for this pattern: pre-fetching of some critical resources at the router level and pre-fetching data in lazy-loaded components.

In the first case, you actually need to fetch data as soon as possible, and you know for sure that the data is critical and required immediately. And lazy-loaded components' JavaScript will be downloaded and executed only when they end up in the render tree, so by definition, after all the critical data is fetched and rendered. So, it's safe.

What if I use libraries for data fetching?

Up until now, in all code examples, I've been using only native `fetch`. This is intentional: I wanted to show you fundamental data fetching patterns in React, and those are libraries-independent. Regardless of any library you're using or want to use, the principle of waterfalls, fetching data within or outside of the React lifecycle remains the same.

React-independent libraries like Axios[28] just abstract away the complexities of dealing with the actual `fetch`, nothing more. I can replace all `fetch` with `axios.get` in the examples, and the result will be the same.

React-integrated libraries with hooks and a query-like API like swr[29] additionally abstract away dealing with `useCallback`, state, and many other things like error handling and caching. Instead of this monstrosity of code that still needs a lot of things to be production-ready:

```
const Comments = () => {
  const [data, setData] = useState();

  useEffect(() => {
    const dataFetch = async () => {
      const data = await (
        await fetch('/get-comments')
      ).json();

      setState(data);
    };
```

```
    dataFetch();
  }, [url]);

  // the rest of comments code
};
```

with swr, I can just write this:

```
const Comments = () => {
  const { data } = useSWR('/get-comments', fetcher);

  // the rest of comments code
};
```

Underneath, all of them will use `useEffect` or equivalent to fetch the data and state to update the data and trigger a re-render of the host component.

What about Suspense?

The data fetching in React story without at least mentioning Suspense would be incomplete. So, what about Suspense? Well, nothing. At the time of publishing the book, Suspense for data fetching is still an undocumented feature[30], not officially supported or recommended by React to use outside of opinionated frameworks like Next.js.

So, if you happen to use one of those frameworks, you'd have to read their documentation on how to use Suspense for data fetching.

But let's imagine that it's available to the general public tomorrow. Will it fundamentally solve data fetching, and will it make everything above obsolete? Not at all.

Suspense is just a really fancy and clever way to replace fiddling with loading states. Instead of this:

```
const Comments = ({ commments }) => {
  if (!comments) return 'loading';

  // render comments
};
```

we're going to lift that loading state up and do this:

```
const Issue = () => {
  return (
    <>
      {/*issue data*/}
      <Suspense fallback="loading">
        <Comments />
      </Suspense>
    </>
```

```
  );
};
```

Everything else, like browser limitations, React lifecycle, and the nature of request waterfalls, stays the same.

Key takeaways

Data fetching on the frontend is a complicated topic. Probably a whole book can be written just about it. In the next chapter, we'll continue the conversation about data fetching and talk about race conditions. But before that, a few things to take away from this chapter:

- We can separate the client's data fetching into two broad categories: initial and on demand.
- We can use the simple `fetch` instead of using data fetching libraries, but a lot of concerns we'd have to implement manually.
- A "performant" app is always subjective and depends on the message we're trying to convey to the users.
- When fetching data, especially initially, we need to be aware of browser limitations on parallel requests.
- Waterfalls appear when we trigger data fetching not in parallel, but conditionally or in sequence.
- We can use techniques such as `Promise.all`, parallel promises, or data providers with Context to avoid waterfalls.
- We can pre-fetch critical resources even before React is initialized, but we need to remember browser limitations while doing so.

Chapter 15. Data fetching and race conditions

Another big topic when it comes to data fetching on the frontend that deserves its own chapter is race conditions. Those are relatively rare in our normal life, and it's possible to develop quite complicated apps without ever having to deal with them. But when they happen, investigating and fixing them can be a real challenge. And since fetch or any async operation in JavaScript is just a glorified Promise most of the time, the main focus of this chapter is Promises.

Let's investigate an app with a race condition, fix it, and in the process learn:

- What Promises are and how very innocent code can create a race condition without us noticing it.
- What are the reasons for race conditions to appear.
- How to fix them in at least four different ways.

What is a Promise?

Before jumping into race conditions themselves, let's remember what a Promise[31] is and why we need them.

Essentially, a Promise is a... promise. When JavaScript executes the code, it usually does so synchronously: step by step. A Promise is one of the very few available ways to execute something asynchronously. With Promises, we can just trigger a task and move on to the next step immediately, without waiting for the task to be done. And the task *promises* that it will notify us when it's completed. And it does! It's very trustworthy.

One of the most important and widely used Promise situations is data fetching. It doesn't matter whether it's the actual `fetch` call or some abstraction on top of it like Axios[32], the Promise behavior is the same.

From the code perspective, it's just this:

```
console.log('first step'); // will log FIRST

fetch('/some-url') // create promise here
  .then(() => {
    // wait for Promise to be done
    // log stuff after the promise is done
    console.log('second step'); // will log THIRD (if successful)
  })
  .catch(() => {
    console.log('something bad happened'); // will log THIRD (if
error happens)
  });

console.log('third step'); // will log SECOND
```

Basically, the flow is: create a promise `fetch('/some-url')` and do something when the result is available in `.then` or handle the error in `.catch`. That's it. There are a few more details to know, of course, to completely master promises[33]. But the core of that flow is enough to understand the rest of the chapter.

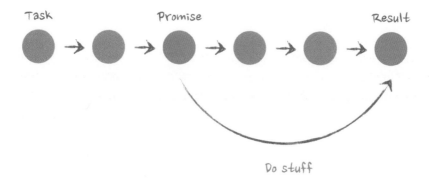

Promises and race conditions

One of the most fun parts of promises is the race conditions they can cause. For this part, I implemented a very simple app to play around with before diving into code.

Interactive example and full code
https://advanced-react.com/examples/15/01

It has a tabs column on the left, navigating between tabs sends a fetch request, and the data from the request is rendered on the right. If we try to navigate between tabs quickly, the experience is bad: the content is blinking and data appears seemingly at random: sometimes the content of the first tab appears, and then quickly replaced by the second tab, sometimes they create some sort of carousel. The whole thing just behaves weird.

The implementation of that app looks something like this. We have two components. One is the root `App` component, which manages the state of the active "page" and renders the navigation buttons and the actual `Page` component.

```
const App = () => {
  const [page, setPage] = useState('1');

  return (
    <>
      {/*left column buttons*/}
      <button onClick={() => setPage('1')}>Issue 1</button>
      <button onClick={() => setPage('2')}>Issue 2</button>

      {/*the actual content*/}
      <Page id={page} />
    </>
  );
};
```

The `Page` component accepts the `id` of the active page as a prop, sends a fetch request to get the data, and then renders it. The simplified implementation (without the loading state) looks like this:

```
const Page = ({ id }: { id: string }) => {
  const [data, setData] = useState({});

  // pass id to fetch relevant data
  const url = `/some-url/${id}`;

  useEffect(() => {
    fetch(url)
      .then((r) => r.json())
      .then((r) => {
        // save data from fetch request to state
        setData(r);
      });
  }, [url]);

  // render data
  return (
    <>
      <h2>{data.title}</h2>
      <p>{data.description}</p>
    </>
  );
};
```

With `id` , we determine the `url` from where to fetch data. Then we're sending the `fetch` request in `useEffect` , and storing the result data in the state - everything is pretty standard. So, where does the race condition and that weird behavior come from?

Race condition reasons

It all comes down to two things: the nature of Promises and the React lifecycle.

From the lifecycle perspective, what happens is this:

- The `App` component is mounted
- The `Page` component is mounted with the default prop value "1"

- useEffect in the Page component kicks in for the first time

Then the nature of Promises comes into effect: fetch within useEffect is a promise, an asynchronous operation. It sends the actual request, and then React just moves on with its life without waiting for the result. After ~2 seconds, the request is done, .then of the promise kicks in, within it we call setData to preserve the data in the state, the Page component is updated with the new data, and we see it on the screen.

If, after everything is rendered and done, I click on the navigation button, we'll have this flow of events:

- The App component changes its state to another page
- The state change triggers a re-render of the App component
- Because of that, the Page component will re-render as well
- useEffect in the Page component has a dependency on id , id has changed, useEffect is triggered again
- fetch in useEffect will be triggered with the new id , after ~2 seconds setData will be called again, the Page component updates, and we'll see the new data on the screen

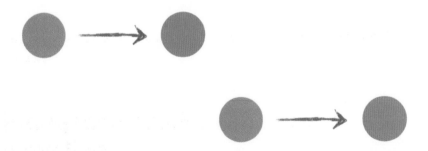

But what will happen if I click on a navigation button and the id changes while the first fetch is in progress and hasn't finished yet? A really cool thing!

- The App component will trigger a re-render of the Page again.
- useEffect will be triggered again (the id has changed!).
- fetch will be triggered again, and React will continue with its business as usual.

- Then, *the first fetch will finish*. It still has the reference to `setData` of the exact same `Page` component (remember - it just updated, so the component is still the same).
- `setData` after the first fetch will be triggered, the `Page` component will update itself with the data from the **first** fetch.
- Then, the second fetch finishes. It was still there, hanging out in the background, as any promise would do. That one also has the reference to exactly the same `setData` of the same `Page` component, it will be triggered, `Page` will again update itself, only this time with the data from the **second** fetch.

Boom, race condition! After navigating to the new page, we see a flash of content: the content from the first finished fetch is rendered, then it's replaced by the content from the second finished fetch.

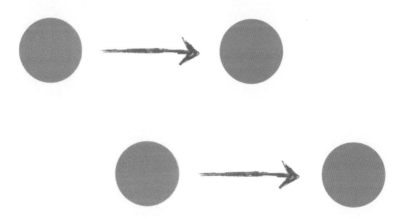

This effect is even more interesting if the second fetch finishes before the first fetch. Then we'll see the correct content of the next page first, and then it will be replaced by the incorrect content of the previous page.

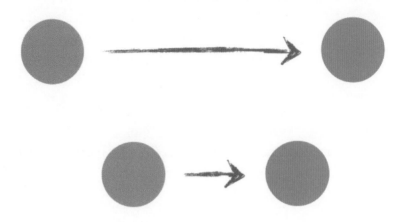

You can see this behavior in the example below. Wait until everything is loaded for the first time, then navigate to the second page, and quickly navigate back to the first page.

Interactive example and full code
https://advanced-react.com/examples/15/02

This is just evil: the code looks innocent, but the app is broken. How to solve it?

Fixing race conditions: force re-mounting

The first solution is not even a solution per se, it's more of an explanation of why these race conditions don't actually happen that often and why we usually don't see them during regular page navigation.

Imagine instead of the implementation above, we had something like this:

```
const App = () => {
  const [page, setPage] = useState('issue');
```

```
  return (
    <>
      {page === 'issue' && <Issue />}
      {page === 'about' && <About />}
    </>
  );
};
```

No passing down props, `Issue` and `About` components have their own unique URLs from which they fetch the data. And the data fetching happens in the `useEffect` hook, exactly the same as before:

```
const About = () => {
  const [about, setAbout] = useState();

  useEffect(() => {
    fetch("/some-url-for-about-page")
      .then((r) => r.json())
      .then((r) => setAbout(r));
  }, []);
  ...
}
```

This time there is no race condition in the app while navigating. Navigate as many times and as fast as you want: it behaves normally.

Interactive example and full code
https://advanced-react.com/examples/15/03

Why?

The answer is here: `{page === 'issue' && <Issue />}`. `Issue` and `About` pages are not re-rendered when the `page` value changes, they are *re-mounted*. When the value changes from `issue` to `about`, the `Issue` component unmounts itself, and the `About` component is mounted in its place.

What is happening from the fetching perspective is this:

- The `App` component renders first, mounts the `Issue` component, data fetching there kicks in.
- When I navigate to the next page while the fetch is still in progress, the `App` component *unmounts* the `Issue` page and mounts the `About` component instead, it kicks off its own data fetching.

And when React unmounts a component, it means it's gone. Gone completely, disappears from the screen, no one has access to it, everything that was happening within, including its state, is lost. Compare this with the previous code, where we wrote `<Page id={page} />`. This `Page` component was never unmounted. We were simply reusing it and its state when navigating.

So, back to the unmounting situation. When the `Issue` 's fetch request finishes while I'm on the `About` page, the `.then` callback of the `Issue` component will try to call its `setIssue` state. But the component is gone. From React's perspective, it doesn't exist anymore. So the promise will just die out, and the data it got will just disappear into the void.

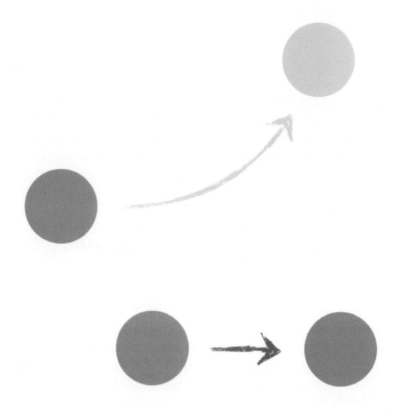

By the way, do you remember that scary warning *"Can't perform a React state update on an unmounted component"*? It used to appear in exactly these situations: when an asynchronous operation like data fetching finishes after the component is already gone. "Used to", since it's gone as well. It was removed quite recently[34].

Anyway. In theory, this behavior can be applied to solve the race condition in the original app: all we need is to force the `Page` component to re-mount on navigation. We can use the "key" attribute for this:

```
<Page id={page} key={page} />
```

As we know from *Chapter 6. Deep dive into diffing and reconciliation*, changing the "key" on an element will force React to remove the one with the "old" key and mount the one with the new "key", even if they are the same type.

However, this is not a solution I would recommend for the general race conditions problem. There are too many caveats: performance might suffer, unexpected bugs with focus and state, unexpected triggering of `useEffect` down the render tree. It's more like sweeping the problem under the rug. There are better ways to deal with race conditions (see below). But it can be a tool in your arsenal in certain cases if used carefully.

Fixing race conditions: drop incorrect result

A much gentler way to solve race conditions, instead of nuking the entire `Page` component from existence, is just to make sure that the result coming in the `.then` callback matches the `id` that is currently "active".

If the result returns the `id` that was used to generate the `url`, we can just compare them. And if they don't match, ignore them. The trick here is to escape the React lifecycle and locally scoped data in functions and get access to the "latest" id inside all iterations of `useEffect`, even the "stale" ones. Yet another use case for Refs, which we discussed in *Chapter 9. Refs: from storing data to imperative API*.

```
const Page = ({ id }) => {
  // create ref
  const ref = useRef(id);

  useEffect(() => {
    // update ref value with the latest id
    ref.current = id;

    fetch(`/some-data-url/${id}`)
      .then((r) => r.json())
      .then((r) => {
```

```
      // compare the latest id with the result
      // only update state if the result actually belongs to that id
      if (ref.current === r.id) {
        setData(r);
      }
    });
  }, [id]);
};
```

Interactive example and full code
https://advanced-react.com/examples/15/04

Your results don't return anything that identifies them reliably? No
problem, we can just compare the url instead:

```
const Page = ({ id }) => {
  // create ref
  const ref = useRef(id);

  useEffect(() => {
    // update ref value with the latest url
    ref.current = url;

    fetch(`/some-data-url/${id}`).then((result) => {
      // compare the latest url with the result's url
      // only update state if the result actually belongs to that url
      if (result.url === ref.current) {
        result.json().then((r) => {
          setData(r);
        });
      }
    });
  }, [url]);
};
```

Interactive example and full code
https://advanced-react.com/examples/15/05

Fixing race conditions: drop all previous results

Don't like the previous solution or think that using a ref for something like this is weird? No problem, there is another way. `useEffect` has something called a "cleanup" function, where we can clean up stuff like subscriptions. Or in our case, it's active fetch requests.

The syntax for it looks like this:

```
// normal useEffect
useEffect(() => {
  // "cleanup" function - function that is returned in useEffect
  return () => {
    // clean something up here
  };
  // dependency - useEffect will be triggered every time url has
changed
}, [url]);
```

The cleanup function[35] is run after a component is unmounted, or *before every re-render with changed dependencies.* So the order of operations during re-render will look like this:

- `url` changes
- "cleanup" function is triggered
- actual content of `useEffect` is triggered

This, along with the nature of JavaScript's functions and closures[36], allows us to do this:

```
useEffect(() => {
  // local variable for useEffect's run
  let isActive = true;

  // do fetch here

  return () => {
    // local variable from above
```

```
      isActive = false;
    };
  }, [url]);
```

We're introducing a local boolean variable `isActive` and setting it to
`true` on `useEffect` run and to `false` on cleanup. The function in
`useEffect` is re-created on every re-render, so the `isActive` for the
latest `useEffect` run will always reset to `true`. But! The "cleanup"
function, which runs before it, still has access to the scope of the *previous
function*, and it will reset it to `false`. This is how JavaScript closures[37]
work.

The `fetch` Promise, although async, still exists only within that closure
and has access only to the local variables of the `useEffect` run that
started it. So when we check the `isActive` boolean in the `.then`
callback, only the latest run, the one that hasn't been cleaned up yet, will
have the variable set to `true`. So all we need now is to check whether
we're in the active closure, and if yes - set state. If no - do nothing. The data
will simply disappear into the void again.

```
useEffect(() => {
  // set this closure to "active"
  let isActive = true;

  fetch(`/some-data-url/${id}`)
    .then((r) => r.json())
    .then((r) => {
      // if the closure is active - update state
      if (isActive) {
        setData(r);
      }
    });

  return () => {
    // set this closure to not active before next re-render
    isActive = false;
  };
}, [id]);
```

Fixing race conditions: cancel all previous requests

Feeling that dealing with JavaScript closures in the context of the React lifecycle makes your brain explode? I'm with you. Sometimes thinking about all of this gives me a headache. But not to worry, there is another option to solve the problem.

Instead of cleaning up or comparing results, we can simply cancel all the previous requests. If they never finish, the state update with obsolete data will never happen, and the problem won't exist. We can use the `AbortController` [38] interface for this.

It's as simple as creating an `AbortController` in `useEffect` and calling `.abort()` in the cleanup function.

```
useEffect(() => {
  // create controller here
  const controller = new AbortController();

  // pass controller as signal to fetch
  fetch(url, { signal: controller.signal })
    .then((r) => r.json())
    .then((r) => {
      setData(r);
    });

  return () => {
    // abort the request here
    controller.abort();
  };
}, [url]);
```

So, on every re-render, the request in progress will be cancelled, and the new one will be the only one allowed to resolve and set state.

Aborting a request in progress will cause the promise to reject, so you'd want to catch errors to get rid of the scary warnings in the console. But handling Promise rejections properly is a good idea regardless of `AbortController`, so it's something you'd want to do with any strategy. Rejecting because of `AbortController` will give a specific type of error, making it easy to exclude it from regular error handling.

```
fetch(url, { signal: controller.signal })
  .then((r) => r.json())
  .then((r) => {
    setData(r);
  })
  .catch((error) => {
    // error because of AbortController
    if (error.name === 'AbortError') {
      // do nothing
    } else {
      // do something, it's a real error!
    }
  });
```

Interactive example and full code
https://advanced-react.com/examples/15/07

Does Async/await change anything?

Nope, not really. Async/await is just a nicer way to write exactly the same promises. It just turns them into "synchronous" functions from the execution flow perspective but doesn't change their asynchronous nature. Instead of:

```
fetch('/some-url')
  .then((r) => r.json())
```

```
  .then((r) => setData(r));
```

We'd write:

```
const response = await fetch('/some-url');
const result = await response.json();
setData(result);
```

Exactly the same app implemented with async/await instead of "traditional" promises will have exactly the same race condition.

> **Interactive example and full code**
> https://advanced-react.com/examples/15/08

And all the solutions and reasons from above apply, just the syntax will be slightly different.

Key takeaways

Hope you're impressed by how cool and innocent-looking race conditions can be and are now able to detect and avoid them with ease. In the final chapter, we'll close the conversation about advanced React patterns with the topic of "what to do if something goes terribly wrong?". But before that, a few things to remember about Promises and race conditions:

- A race condition can happen when we update state multiple times after a promise is resolved in the same React component.

```
useEffect(() => {
  fetch(url)
    .then((r) => r.json())
    .then((r) => {
      // this is vulnerable to the race conditions
      setData(r);
    });
```

```
}, [url]);
```

- We can fix it by:
  - ○ Forcing a re-mount of a component with the "old" data that we don't need.
  - ○ Comparing the returned result with the variable that triggered the promise and not setting state if they don't match.
  - ○ Tracing the latest promise via the clean-up function in the `useEffect` and dropping the result of all "old" promises.
  - ○ Using `AbortController` to cancel all previous requests.

Chapter 16. Universal error handling in React

We all want our apps to be stable, work perfectly, and cater to every edge case imaginable, don't we? But the sad reality is that we are all humans (at least that is my assumption), we all make mistakes, and there is no such thing as bug-free code. No matter how careful we are or how many automated tests we write, there will always be a situation when something goes terribly wrong. The important thing, when it comes to user experience, is to predict that terrible thing, localize it as much as possible, and deal with it in a graceful way until it can be actually fixed.

In the final chapter, let's take a look at error handling in React:

- What we can do if an error happens.
- What the caveats of different approaches to error catching are.
- How to mitigate them.

Why we should catch errors in React

But first things first: why is it vitally important to have some error-catching solution in React?

The answer is simple: starting from version 16, an error thrown during the React lifecycle will cause the entire app to unmount itself if not stopped. Before that, components would be preserved on the screen, even if malformed and misbehaved. Now, an unfortunate uncaught error in some insignificant part of the UI, or even some external library that you have no control over, can destroy the entire page and render an empty screen for everyone.

Never before had frontend developers such destructive power!

Remembering how to catch errors in JavaScript

When it comes to catching those nasty surprises in regular JavaScript, the tools are pretty straightforward.

We have our good old `try/catch` [39] statement, which is more or less self-explanatory: `try` to do stuff, and if they fail - `catch` the mistake and do something to mitigate it:

```
try {
  // if we're doing something wrong, this might throw an error
  doSomething();
} catch (e) {
  // if error happened, catch it and do something with it without
stopping the app
  // like sending this error to some logging service
}
```

This also works with `async` functions with the same syntax:

```
try {
  await fetch('/bla-bla');
} catch (e) {
  // oh no, the fetch failed! We should do something about it!
}
```

Or, if we're going with old-school promises, we have a `catch` method specifically for them. So if we rewrite the previous `fetch` example with a promise-based API, it will look like this:

```
fetch('/bla-bla')
  .then((result) => {
    // if a promise is successful, the result will be here
    // we can do something useful with it
  })
  .catch((e) => {
    // oh no, the fetch failed! We should do something about it!
```

```
  });
```

It's the same concept, just a bit different implementation, so for the rest of the chapter, I'm just going to use `try/catch` syntax for all errors.

Simple try/catch in React: how to and caveats

When an error is caught, we need to do something with it, right? So, what exactly can we do, other than logging it somewhere? Or, to be more precise: what can we do for our users? Just leaving them with an empty screen or broken interface is not exactly user-friendly.

The most obvious and intuitive answer would be to render something while we wait for the fix. Luckily, we can do whatever we want in that `catch` statement, including setting the state. So we can do something like this:

```
const SomeComponent = () => {
  const [hasError, setHasError] = useState(false);

  useEffect(() => {
    try {
      // do something like fetching some data
    } catch (e) {
      // oh no! the fetch failed, we have no data to render!
      setHasError(true);
    }
  });

  // something happened during fetch, lets render some nice error
screen
  if (hasError) return <SomeErrorScreen />;

  // all's good, data is here, let's render it
  return <SomeComponentContent {...datasomething} />;
};
```

We're trying to send a fetch request, if it fails - setting the error state, and if the error state is `true` , then we render an error screen with some additional info for users, like a support contact number.

This approach is pretty straightforward and works great for simple, predictable, and narrow use cases like catching a failed `fetch` request.

But if you want to catch all errors that can happen in a component, you'll face some challenges and serious limitations.

Limitation 1: you will have trouble with the useEffect hook.

If we wrap `useEffect` with `try/catch` , it simply won't work:

```
try {
  useEffect(() => {
    throw new Error('Hulk smash!');
  }, []);
} catch (e) {
  // useEffect throws, but this will never be called
}
```

This happens because `useEffect` is called asynchronously after rendering, so from the `try/catch` perspective, everything went successfully. It's the same story as with any Promise, which we discussed in *Chapter 15. Data fetching and race conditions*: if we don't wait for the result, then JavaScript will continue with its business, return to it when the promise is done, and only execute what is *inside* `useEffect` (or then of a Promise). `try/catch` block will be executed and long gone by then.

In order for errors inside `useEffect` to be caught, try/catch should be placed *inside* as well:

```
useEffect(() => {
  try {
    throw new Error('Hulk smash!');
  } catch (e) {
    // this one will be caught
  }
```

```
}, []);
```

Interactive example and full code
https://advanced-react.com/examples/16/01

This applies to any hook that uses `useEffect` or to anything asynchronous really. As a result, instead of just one `try/catch` that wraps everything, you'd have to split it into multiple blocks: one for each hook.

Limitation 2: children components.

`try/catch` won't be able to catch anything that happens inside children components. You can't just do this:

```
const Component = () => {
  let child;

  try {
    child = <Child />;
  } catch (e) {
    // useless for catching errors inside Child component, won't be
triggered
  }

  return child;
};
```

or even this:

```
const Component = () => {
  try {
    return <Child />;
  } catch (e) {
    // still useless for catching errors inside Child component,
won't be triggered
  }
};
```

This happens because when we write `<Child />` , we're not actually rendering this component. What we're doing is creating a component `Element` , which is nothing more than a component's *definition*. It's just an object that contains necessary information like component type and props that will be used later by React itself, which will actually trigger the render of this component. We discussed this in detail in *Chapter 2. Elements, children as props, and re-renders, Chapter 3. Configuration concerns with elements as props*, and *Chapter 6. Deep dive into diffing and reconciliation*.

And the render will happen *after* the `try/catch` block is executed successfully, exactly the same story as with promises and the `useEffect` hook.

Limitation 3: Setting state during render is a no-no

If you're trying to catch errors outside of `useEffect` and various callbacks (i.e., during the component's render), then dealing with them properly is not that trivial anymore: state updates during render are not allowed.

Simple code like this, for example, will cause an infinite loop of re-renders if an error happens:

```
const Component = () => {
  const [hasError, setHasError] = useState(false);

  try {
    doSomethingComplicated();
  } catch (e) {
    // don't do that! will cause infinite loop in case of an error
    // see codesandbox below with live example
    setHasError(true);
  }
```

```
};
```

Interactive example and full code
https://advanced-react.com/examples/16/03

We could, of course, just return the error screen here instead of setting
state:

```
const Component = () => {
  try {
    doSomethingComplicated();
  } catch (e) {
    // this allowed
    return <SomeErrorScreen />;
  }
};
```

But this, as you can imagine, is a bit cumbersome and forces us to handle
errors in the same component differently: state for useEffect and
callbacks, and direct return for everything else.

```
// while it will work, it's super cumbersome and hard to maitain,
don't do that
const SomeComponent = () => {
  const [hasError, setHasError] = useState(false);

  useEffect(() => {
    try {
      // do something like fetching some data
    } catch (e) {
      // can't just return in case of errors in useEffect or callbacks
      // so have to use state
      setHasError(true);
    }
  });

  try {
    // do something during render
```

```
  } catch (e) {
    // but here we can't use state, so have to return directly in
case of an error
    return <SomeErrorScreen />;
  }

  // and still have to return in case of error state here
  if (hasError) return <SomeErrorScreen />;

  return <SomeComponentContent {...datasomething} />;
};
```

To summarize this section: if we rely solely on `try/catch` in React, we
will either miss most of the errors or turn every component into an
incomprehensible mess of code that will probably cause errors by itself.

Fortunately, there is another way.

React ErrorBoundary component

To mitigate the limitations from above, React gives us what is known as
"Error Boundaries"[40]: a special API that turns a regular component into a
`try/catch` statement in a way, only for React declarative code. Typical
usage that you can see in every example over there, including the React
docs, will be something like this:

```
const Component = () => {
  return (
    <ErrorBoundary>
      <SomeChildComponent />
      <AnotherChildComponent />
    </ErrorBoundary>
  );
};
```

Now, if something goes wrong in any of those components or their children
during render, the error will be caught and dealt with.

But React doesn't give us the component *per se*, it just gives us a tool to implement it. The simplest implementation would look something like this:

```
class ErrorBoundary extends React.Component {
  constructor(props) {
    super(props);
    // initialize the error state
    this.state = { hasError: false };
  }

  // if an error happened, set the state to true
  static getDerivedStateFromError(error) {
    return { hasError: true };
  }

  render() {
    // if error happened, return a fallback component
    if (this.state.hasError) {
      return <>Oh no! Epic fail!</>;
    }

    return this.props.children;
  }
}
```

We create a regular class component (going old-school here, no hooks for error boundaries available) and implement the `getDerivedStateFromError` method - this turns the component into a proper error boundary.

Another important thing to do when dealing with errors is to send the error info somewhere where it can wake up everyone who's on-call. For this, error boundaries give us the `componentDidCatch` method:

```
class ErrorBoundary extends React.Component {
  // everything else stays the same

  componentDidCatch(error, errorInfo) {
    // send error to somewhere here
    log(error, errorInfo);
```

```
    }
  }
```

After the error boundary is set up, we can do whatever we want with it, same as any other component. We can, for example, make it more reusable and pass the fallback as a prop:

```
render() {
  // if error happened, return a fallback component
  if (this.state.hasError) {
    return this.props.fallback;
  }

  return this.props.children;
}
```

And use it like this:

```
const Component = () => {
  return (
    <ErrorBoundary fallback={<>Oh no! Do something!</>}>
      <SomeChildComponent />
      <AnotherChildComponent />
    </ErrorBoundary>
  );
};
```

Or anything else that we might need, like resetting state on a button click, differentiating between types of errors, or pushing that error to a context somewhere.

Interactive example and full code
https://advanced-react.com/examples/16/04

There is one caveat in this error-free world though: it doesn't catch *everything*.

ErrorBoundary component: limitations

Error boundaries only catch errors that happen during the React lifecycle.
Things that happen outside of it, like resolved promises, async code with
`setTimeout` , various callbacks, and event handlers, will disappear if not
dealt with explicitly.

```
const Component = () => {
  useEffect(() => {
    // this one will be caught by ErrorBoundary component
    throw new Error('Destroy everything!');
  }, []);

  const onClick = () => {
    // this error will just disappear into the void
    throw new Error('Hulk smash!');
  };

  useEffect(() => {
    // if this one fails, the error will also disappear
    fetch('/bla');
  }, []);

  return <button onClick={onClick}>click me</button>;
};

const ComponentWithBoundary = () => {
  return (
    <ErrorBoundary>
      <Component />
    </ErrorBoundary>
  );
};
```

The common recommendation here is to use regular `try/catch` for these
types of errors. And at least here we can use state safely (more or less):
callbacks of event handlers are exactly the places where we usually set state
anyway. So technically, we can just combine two approaches and do
something like this:

```
const Component = () => {
  const [hasError, setHasError] = useState(false);

  // most of the errors in this component and in children will be
  caught by the ErrorBoundary

  const onClick = () => {
    try {
      // this error will be caught by catch
      throw new Error('Hulk smash!');
    } catch (e) {
      setHasError(true);
    }
  };

  if (hasError) return 'something went wrong';

  return <button onClick={onClick}>click me</button>;
};

const ComponentWithBoundary = () => {
  return (
    <ErrorBoundary fallback={'Oh no! Something went wrong'}>
      <Component />
    </ErrorBoundary>
  );
};
```

But. We're back to square one: every component needs to maintain its "error" state and, more importantly, make a decision on what to do with it.

We can, of course, instead of dealing with those errors on a component level, just propagate them up to the parent that has `ErrorBoundary` via props or `Context`. This way, at least we can have a "fallback" component in just one place:

```
const Component = ({ onError }) => {
  const onClick = () => {
    try {
      throw new Error('Hulk smash!');
```

```
    } catch (e) {
      // just call a prop instead of maintaining state here
      onError();
    }
  };

  return <button onClick={onClick}>click me</button>;
};

const ComponentWithBoundary = () => {
  const [hasError, setHasError] = useState();
  const fallback = 'Oh no! Something went wrong';

  if (hasError) return fallback;

  return (
    <ErrorBoundary fallback={fallback}>
      <Component onError={() => setHasError(true)} />
    </ErrorBoundary>
  );
};
```

But it's so much additional code! We'd have to do it for every child
component in the render tree. Not to mention that we're basically
maintaining two error states now: one in the parent component and
another in `ErrorBoundary` itself. And `ErrorBoundary` already has all
the mechanisms in place to propagate the errors up the tree, so we're doing
double work here.

Can't we just catch those errors from async code and event handlers with
`ErrorBoundary` instead?

Catching async errors with ErrorBoundary

Interestingly enough, we actually can catch all errors with
`ErrorBoundary` ! There is a cool trick to achieve exactly that[41].

The trick here is to catch those errors first with `try/catch`. Then inside the `catch` statement, trigger a normal React re-render, and then re-throw those errors back into the re-render lifecycle. That way, `ErrorBoundary` can catch them like any other error. And since a state update is the way to trigger a re-render, and the state set function can actually accept an updater function[42] as an argument, the solution is pure magic:

```
const Component = () => {
  // create some random state that we'll use to throw errors
  const [state, setState] = useState();

  const onClick = () => {
    try {
      // something bad happened
    } catch (e) {
      // trigger state update, with updater function as an argument
      setState(() => {
        // re-throw this error within the updater function
        // it will be triggered during state update
        throw e;
      });
    }
  };
};
```

Interactive example and full code
https://advanced-react.com/examples/16/05

The final step here would be to abstract this hack away so we don't have to create random states in every component. We can get creative here and make a hook that gives us an async error thrower:

```
const useThrowAsyncError = () => {
  const [state, setState] = useState();

  return (error) => {
    setState(() => throw error)
```

```
  }
}
```

And use it like this:

```
const Component = () => {
  const throwAsyncError = useThrowAsyncError();

  useEffect(() => {
    fetch('/bla')
      .then()
      .catch((e) => {
        // throw async error here!
        throwAsyncError(e);
      });
  });
};
```

Or, we can create a wrapper for callbacks like this:

```
const useCallbackWithErrorHandling = (callback) => {
  const [state, setState] = useState();

  return (...args) => {
    try {
      callback(...args);
    } catch(e) {
      setState(() => throw e);
    }
  }
}
```

And use it like this:

```
const Component = () => {
  const onClick = () => {
    // do something dangerous here
  };
```

```
  const onClickWithErrorHandler =
    useCallbackWithErrorHandling(onClick);

  return (
    <button onClick={onClickWithErrorHandler}>
      click me!
    </button>
  );
};
```

Or anything else that your heart desires and the app requires. There are no limits! And no errors will get away anymore.

Interactive example and full code
https://advanced-react.com/examples/16/06

Can I just use the react-error-boundary library instead?

For those of you who hate reinventing the wheel or just prefer libraries for already solved problems, there is a nice library called "react-error-boundary"[43] that implements a flexible `ErrorBoundary` component and has a few useful utils similar to those described above.

Whether to use it or not is just a matter of personal preferences, coding style, and unique situations within your components.

Key takeaways

That is it for the errors and this chapter, and in fact this book! Hope this was an enjoyable experience for you. And don't forget, when dealing with errors in React:

- Uncaught errors in the React lifecycle after version 16 will unmount the entire app. So at least a few ErrorBoundaries in strategic places are non-negotiable.

- A simple `try/catch` will catch errors in callbacks or in promises just fine, but it won't be able to catch errors that are coming from any nested components, and you won't be able to wrap `useEffect` or the return of the component in `try/catch` .
- The ErrorBoundary component is the opposite. It will catch errors originated in any component down the render tree, but it will skip promises and callbacks (anything async).
- We can merge them together and create an uber ErrorBoundary component if we catch the `async` errors with `try/catch` and re-throw them into the normal React lifecycle.
- We can either implement a simple `useAsyncError` hook for that or just use the `react-error-boundary` library, which operates on similar principles.

Forewords

That's a wrap! Congratulations, you've made it! Hope it was worth the time spent, you learned plenty of new things, and most importantly, had fun while doing so.

If you have any feedback, please don't hesitate to share it at feedback@advanced-react.com.

Feel free to follow and connect with the author on LinkedIn (https://www.linkedin.com/in/adevnadia/) and Twitter, or whatever the name of that platform is going to be by the time the book is published (https://twitter.com/adevnadia).

Read the author's blog for more content like in this book: https://www.developerway.com

Subscribe to the newsletter for updates on new product releases. There may or may not be a video course coming on the topic of this book ;): https://www.advanced-react.com

Cheers and g'day,

Nadia

Footnotes

[1] React.createEement function documentation:
https://reactjs.org/docs/react-api.html#createelement

[2] React.cloneElement function documentation:
https://react.dev/reference/react/cloneElement

[3] Real implementation of useMemo hook:
https://github.com/facebook/react/blob/main/packages/react-reconciler/src/ReactFiberHooks.js#L2273

[4] DOM documentation: https://developer.mozilla.org/en-US/docs/Web/API/Document_Object_Model/Introduction

[5] JavaScript appendChild documentation:
https://developer.mozilla.org/en-US/docs/Web/API/Node/appendChild

[6] Higher-Order Components in React documentation:
https://reactjs.org/docs/higher-order-components.html

[7] Redux 'connect' documentation: https://react-redux.js.org/api/connect

[8] React router 'withRouter' documentation:
https://v5.reactrouter.com/web/api/withRouter

[9] useImperativeHandle documentation:
https://react.dev/reference/react/useImperativeHandle

[10] React.memo comparison function documentation:
https://react.dev/reference/react/memo#specifying-a-custom-comparison-function

[11] Lodash library: https://lodash.com/

[12] Debouncing and throttling explained: https://css-tricks.com/debouncing-throttling-explained-examples/

[13] Implementation of 'debounce' function in lodash:
https://github.com/lodash/lodash/blob/master/debounce.js

[14] useLayoutEffect documentation:
https://react.dev/reference/react/useLayoutEffect

[15] You Might Not Need an Effect: https://react.dev/learn/you-might-not-need-an-effect

[16] 'postMessage' and 'requestAnimationFrame' trick in React:
https://stackoverflow.com/questions/56727477/react-how-does-react-make-sure-that-useeffect-is-called-after-the-browser-has-h/56727837#56727837

[17] CSS 'position' property: https://developer.mozilla.org/en-US/docs/Web/CSS/position

[18] Stacking Context documentation: https://developer.mozilla.org/en-US/docs/Web/CSS/CSS_positioned_layout/Understanding_z-index/Stacking_context

[19] Stacking Context documentation: https://developer.mozilla.org/en-US/docs/Web/CSS/CSS_positioned_layout/Understanding_z-index/Stacking_context

[20] Containing Block documentation: https://developer.mozilla.org/en-US/docs/Web/CSS/Containing_block

[21] How React responds to events, documentation:
https://react.dev/learn/responding-to-events#event-propagation

[22] Explanation of submit event behavior in React:
https://github.com/facebook/react/issues/22470

[23] Axios library: https://github.com/axios/axios

[24] swr library: https://swr.vercel.app/docs/getting-started

[25] Chrome network documentation:
https://developer.chrome.com/docs/devtools/network/reference/?utm_source=devtools#timing-explanation

[26] Promise.all documentation: https://developer.mozilla.org/en-US/docs/Web/JavaScript/Reference/Global_Objects/Promise/all

[27] Promise documentation: https://developer.mozilla.org/en-US/docs/Web/JavaScript/Reference/Global_Objects/Promise

[28] Axios library: https://github.com/axios/axios

[29] swr library: https://swr.vercel.app/docs/getting-started

[30] Suspense documentation: https://react.dev/reference/react/Suspense

[31] Promise documentation: https://developer.mozilla.org/en-US/docs/Web/JavaScript/Reference/Global_Objects/Promise

[32] Axios library: https://github.com/axios/axios

[33] Promise documentation: https://developer.mozilla.org/en-US/docs/Web/JavaScript/Reference/Global_Objects/Promise

[34] Issue on github: https://github.com/facebook/react/pull/22114

[35] useEffect cleanup function: https://react.dev/reference/react/useEffect#my-cleanup-logic-runs-even-though-my-component-didnt-unmount

[36] Closures documentation: https://developer.mozilla.org/en-US/docs/Web/JavaScript/Closures

[37] JavaScript Closure documentation: https://developer.mozilla.org/en-US/docs/Web/JavaScript/Closures

[38] AbortController documentation: https://developer.mozilla.org/en-US/docs/Web/API/AbortController

[39] try...catch documentation: https://developer.mozilla.org/en-US/docs/Web/JavaScript/Reference/Statements/try...catch

[40] ErrorBoundaries documentation: https://reactjs.org/docs/error-boundaries.html

[41] Dan Abramov describes the ErrorBoundary async trick:
https://github.com/facebook/react/issues/14981#issuecomment-468460187

[42] Updater function documentation:
https://react.dev/reference/react/useState#updating-state-based-on-the-previous-state

[43] react-error-boundary library: https://github.com/bvaughn/react-error-boundary